Berklee Practice Method

VIBRAPHONE

Get Your Band Together

ED SAINDON
and the
Berklee Faculty

T0034059

Berklee Media

Associate Vice President: Dave Kusek
Director of Content: Debbie Cavalier
Business Manager: Linda Chady Chase
Technology Manager: Mike Serio
Marketing Manager, Berkleemusic: Barry Kelly
Senior Designer: David Ehlers

Berklee Press

Sr. Writer/Editor: Jonathan Feist
Writer/Editor: Susan Gedutis
Production Manager: Shawn Girsberger
Marketing Manager, Berklee Press: Jennifer Rassler
Product Marketing Manager: David Goldberg

ISBN 0-634-00794-7

1140 Boylston Street
Boston, MA 02215-3693 USA
(617) 747-2146

Visit Berklee Press Online at
www.berkleepress.com

DISTRIBUTED BY

HAL•LEONARD®
CORPORATION
7777 W. BLUEMOUND RD. P.O. BOX 13819
MILWAUKEE, WISCONSIN 53213

Visit Hal Leonard Online at
www.halleonard.com

DESIGN TEAM

Matt Marvuglio	Curriculum Editor
	Dean of the Professional Performance Division
Jonathan Feist	Series Editor
	Senior Writer/Editor, Berklee Press

Rich Appleman	Chair of the Bass Department
Larry Baione	Chair of the Guitar Department
Jeff Galindo	Assistant Professor of Brass
Matt Glaser	Chair of the String Department
Russell Hoffmann	Assistant Professor of Piano
Charles Lewis	Associate Professor of Brass
Jim Odgren	Academic Advising Coordinator
Tiger Okoshi	Assistant Professor of Brass
Bill Pierce	Chair of the Woodwind Department
Tom Plsek	Chair of the Brass Department
Mimi Rabson	Assistant Professor of Strings
John Repucci	Assistant Chair of the Bass Department
Ed Saindon	Professor of Percussion
Ron Savage	Chair of the Ensemble Department
Casey Scheuerell	Associate Professor of Percussion
Paul Schmeling	Chair of the Piano Department

The Band

Rich Appleman, Bass
Larry Baione, Guitar
Ed Saindon, Vibraphone
Casey Scheuerell, Drums
Paul Schmeling, Keyboard

Music composed by Matt Marvuglio
Recording produced and engineered by Rob Jaczko, Chair of the Music Production and
    Engineering Department

Contents

CD Tracks

Chapter I. Playing Rock ("Sweet")

CD 1. "Sweet" Full Band

CD 2. "Sweet" First Part

CD 3. "Sweet" Second Part

CD 4. "Sweet" Comping

CD 5. "Sweet" Vibraphone/Bass

CD 6. "Sweet" You're the Vibraphone

CD 7. "Sweet" Call/Response 1

CD 8. "Sweet" Call/Response 2

Chapter II. Playing Blues ("Do It Now")

CD 9. "Do It Now" Full Band

CD 10. "Do It Now" You're the Vibraphone

CD 11. "Do It Now" Call/Response 1

CD 12. "Do It Now" Call/Response 2

CD 13. "Do It Now" Call/Response 3

CD 14. "Do It Now" Call/Response 4

Chapter III. Playing Blues Swing ("I Just Wanna Be With You")

CD 15. "I Just Wanna Be With You" Full Band

CD 16. "I Just Wanna Be With You" You're the Vibraphone

CD 17. "I Just Wanna Be With You" Call/Response 1

CD 18. "I Just Wanna Be With You" Call/Response 2

Chapter IV. Playing Funk ("Leave Me Alone")

CD 19. "Leave Me Alone" Full Band

CD 20. "Leave Me Alone" Call/Response 1

CD 21. "Leave Me Alone" Call/Response 2

CD 22. "Leave Me Alone" You're the Vibraphone

CD 23. "Leave Me Alone" Call/Response 3

CD 24. "Leave Me Alone" Call/Response 4

Foreword

Berklee College of Music has been training musicians for over fifty years. Our graduates go onto successful careers in the music business, and many have found their way to the very top of the industry, producing hit records, receiving the highest awards, and sharing their music with millions of people.

An important reason why Berklee is so successful is that our curriculum stresses the practical application of musical principles. Our students spend a lot of time playing together in bands. When you play with other musicians, you learn things that are impossible to learn in any other way. Teachers are invaluable, practicing by yourself is critical, but performing in a band is the most valuable experience of all. That's what is so special about this series: it gives you the theory you need, but also prepares you to play in a band.

The goal of the *Berklee Practice Method* is to present some of Berklee's teaching strategies in book and audio form. The chairs of each of our instrumental departments—guitar, bass, keyboard, percussion, woodwind, brass, and string—have gotten together and discussed the best ways to teach you how to play in a band. They teamed with some of our best faculty and produced a set of books with play-along audio tracks that uniquely prepares its readers to play with other musicians.

Students who want to study at Berklee come from a variety of backgrounds. Some have great technique, but have never improvised. Some have incredible ears, but need more work on their reading skills. Some have a very creative, intuitive sense of music, but their technical skills aren't strong enough, yet, to articulate their ideas.

The *Berklee Practice Method* teaches many of these different aspects of musicianship. It is the material that our faculty wishes all Berklee freshmen could master before arriving on our doorstep.

When you work through this book, don't just read it. You've got to play through every example, along with the recording. Better yet, play them with your own band.

Playing music with other people is how you will learn the most. This series will help you master the skills you need to become a creative, expressive, and supportive musician that anyone would want to have in their band.

Gary Burton
Executive Vice President,
Berklee College of Music

Preface

Thank you for choosing the *Berklee Practice Method* for vibraphone. This book/CD package, developed by the faculty of Berklee College of Music, is part of the *Berklee Practice Method* series—the instrumental method that teaches how to play in a band.

The recording included with this method provides an instant band you can play along with, featuring great players from Berklee's performance faculty. Each tune has exercises and practice tracks that will help prepare you to play it. Rock, blues, and funk are just some of the styles you will perform.

The lessons in this book will guide you through technique that is specific to playing a keyboard instrument in a contemporary ensemble. When you play in a band, your primary concern is with chords—how to read and play them, how to progress from one to the next, and how they interact with other instruments, melodically and rhythmically. This is very different than traditional classical playing, and it will be a major part of this method. This book is intended for vibraphone players who know how to read notes and basic rhythms, and play all major scales and some arpeggios. (These are summarized in the first chapter.) Ideally, this method should be learned under the guidance of a private teacher, but vibraphone players learning on their own will also find it invaluable.

Most important, you will learn the skills you need to play vibraphone in a band. Play along with the recording, and play with your friends. This series coordinates methods for many different instruments, and all are based on the same tunes, in the same keys. If you know a drummer, guitarist, horn player, etc., have them pick up the *Berklee Practice Method* for their own instruments, and then you can jam together.

Work hard, make music, have fun!

Ed Saindon
Professor of Percussion
Berklee College of Music

Basics

Before you start chapter 1, you should understand the following topics.

MALLET TECHNIQUE

Two styles of vibe playing have evolved throughout the history of the vibraphone. The two-mallet approach was first used by Lionel Hampton and Milt Jackson beginning in the 1930s. In this style, the vibraphone is primarily a melodic instrument and imitates more horn-like instruments, such as trumpet and saxophone. The four-mallet approach, as pioneered by Gary Burton in the 1960s, uses the instrument harmonically as well as melodically.

The use of four mallets affords the use of chords along with melody. In this way, you can play melodies as well as accompany. For this book, you should use the four-mallet technique, as you will be playing both chords and melodies.

This hand position will give you the best balance and control.

Bottom View　　　　　　　　　　　　　**Top View**

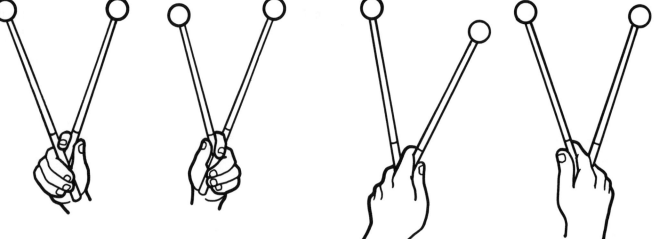

When you stand at the vibes, your instrument should be at a height that is comfortable to you. Your right foot should always rest on the pedal. A good teacher is essential to learning good posture and hand position.

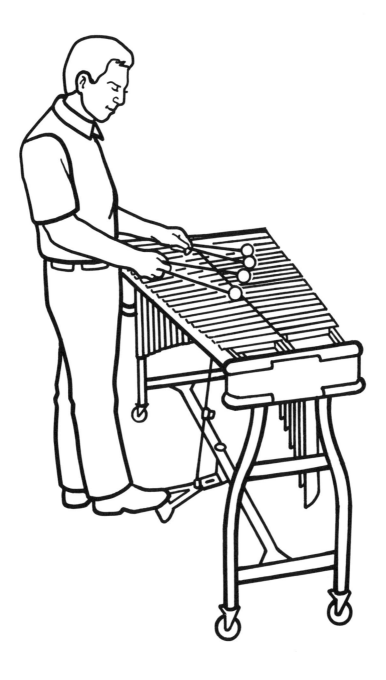

MICROPHONES

If you use microphones to amplify your vibes, generally you should use two mics (mounted on booms) pointing down at the instrument. Center one over the bass section of the vibes and one over the treble section. To protect your equipment and your ear drums, follow these steps when you plug your mics into an amp or mixing board.

1. Turn off the amp and set the volume down to 0.

2. Plug your cable into your mics and then into the amp.

3. Turn on the amp.

4. Play at a medium volume. Slowly, turn up the amp volume on each channel until it is loud enough. Make sure that they are balanced with each other so that the entire instrument plays at an even volume. If you get any feedback, turn down the volume or change the mic position until it stops.

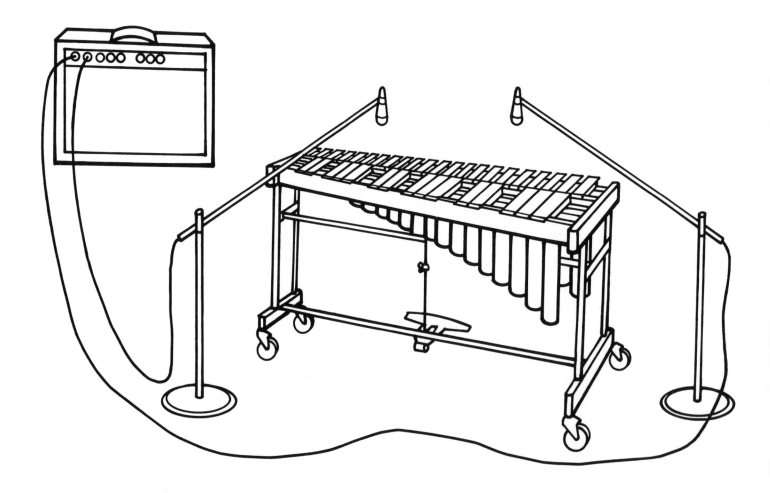

NOTATION

Notes are written on a staff.

LEDGER LINES

The staff can be extended with ledger lines.

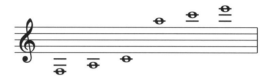

ACCIDENTALS

Accidentals are symbols appearing before notes, showing that a pitch is raised or lowered for the duration of the measure, unless otherwise indicated.

♭	Flat	Next note down (half step)
♯	Sharp	Next note up (half step)
♮	Natural	Cancels a flat or sharp

SCALES: MAJOR AND MINOR

Scales are patterns of notes, presented sequentially in a single octave. Two common types of scales are the major and minor scales.

KEY SIGNATURES

Key signatures indicate a tune's key and show which notes always get sharps or flats. Accidentals on the lines and spaces in the key signature affect those notes unless there is a natural sign. Here are some key signatures used in this book.

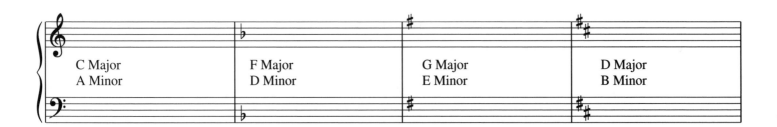

RHYTHMS

Here are some basic rhythms. When there are no actual pitches, as in a clapping exercise, rhythms may be shown on the *percussion clef*. (The beats are numbered below the staff.)

Percussion Clef

Connect notes using a tie. The first note is held for a total of six beats.

Extend a note's rhythmic value by using a dot. A dot increases the value by one half.

Triplets squeeze three even attacks into the space of two. In this example, the quarter-note beat is divided first into two eighth notes, and then into three eighth-note triplets.

RHYTHMIC NOTATION

Music that just shows rhythms may be written in rhythmic notation. This is common for rhythm exercises when you clap or tap your foot, without sounding any specific pitches.

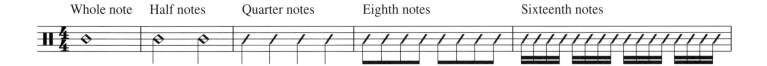

MEASURES

Groups of beats are divided into measures. Measure lengths are shown with *time signatures.*
This measure is in $\frac{4}{4}$ time—there are four quarter notes in the measure.

In $\frac{12}{8}$ time, there are twelve eighth notes per measure.

ARTICULATIONS

Articulations give more information about how to play a note. Here are four common ones used in this book:

>	Accent	Loud
.	Staccato	Short
^	Short Accent	Short and loud
–	Long	Hold for full value

Now, let's play!

"Sweet" is a *rock* tune. Rock started in the 1960s and has roots in blues, swing, r&b, and rock 'n' roll. There are many different styles of rock. To hear more rock, listen to artists such as Rage Against the Machine, Melissa Etheridge, Korn, Paula Cole, Bjork, Tori Amos, Primus, Jimi Hendrix, Led Zeppelin, and vibraphonist Roy Ayers.

LESSON 1
TECHNIQUE/THEORY

Listen to "Sweet" on the recording. This tune has two main parts. The vibe part is shown below with notes only, no rhythms.

In the first part, the vibraphone plays these chords:

In the second part, the vibraphone plays these chords:

Play along with the recording, and try to match the vibraphone, which doubles with the keyboard. Notice that there is a short introduction before the first part begins.

CHORDS

The vibe part you just played was made up of *chords* (three or more notes played at the same time). "Sweet" has two kinds of chords: *major* and *minor*. These chords are built using notes of the major or minor scale. In this tune, the chords are *triads* (chords with three notes, besides any octave doublings).

In the first part, the first chord you played was an E minor triad. It is built using the first, third, and fifth notes of the E minor scale.

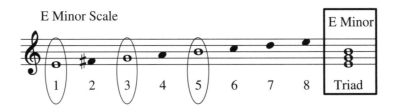

The second chord you played was an A major triad. It is built using the first, third, and fifth notes of the A major scale.

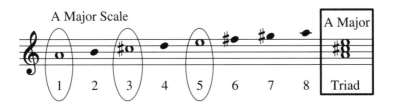

LISTEN **2** PLAY

Play the chords along with the first part to "Sweet." Listen to the different qualities of the two chords.

CHORD SYMBOLS

Chords are often represented by *chord symbols*. *Major chords* use just the chord's letter (A). *Minor chords* add a long dash (E–) to the letter (or sometimes, a lowercase "m" or "min" instead of the dash).

The second part to "Sweet" uses two different chords: A minor and D major.

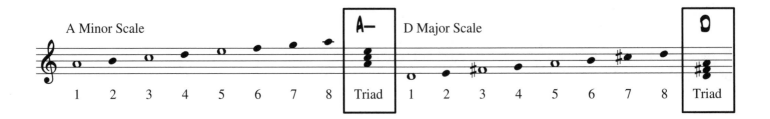

LISTEN **3** PLAY

Play along with the second part of "Sweet." Here are the notes and chord symbols.

LEAD SHEETS

When you play in a band, your sheet music might show just chord symbols and melody. This is called a *lead sheet*. Lead sheets tell which chords to play along with the melody. The whole band may read the same lead sheet. Each player will use it differently to create a part for their instrument. As a vibraphone player, you will use the lead sheet to learn which chords to play.

This is what the first part of "Sweet" looks like on a lead sheet:

This is what the lead sheet looks like for the second part:

You will see the full lead sheet to "Sweet" in lesson 4.

PERFORMANCE TIP

You may notice that the chord notes next to the scales are stacked in a different order than the chords in the notated parts. Lead sheet notation lets you decide how to arrange the chord notes. It also lets you choose your own rhythms to play these chords. When you read off a lead sheet, you can play the chords however you want, as long as your part fits in, or *hooks up*, with what the rest of the band is playing.

Different vibraphone players will create different parts to the same tune. This is one of the coolest things about lead sheet notation: it leaves room for individual interpretation.

LESSON 2
LEARNING THE GROOVE

WHAT IS A GROOVE?

A *groove* is a combination of musical patterns in which everyone in the band feels and plays to a common pulse. This creates a sense of unity and momentum. The *rhythm section* (usually drums, bass, and an instrument that can play chords, such as vibraphone, keyboard, or guitar) lays down the groove's dynamic and rhythmic feel. A singer or soloist also contributes to the groove and performs the melody based on this feel.

Listen to "Sweet." As is common in hard rock, the groove to "Sweet" has a strong, clear pulse, and a loud, forceful sound. The drums play a heavy, repetitive beat. The bass outlines the harmonic structure. The guitar, keyboards, and vibraphone play chords. Everyone uses the same rhythms, though often at different times. This makes the whole band sound like one unit, or *hooked up* with the groove.

In lesson 1, when you played along with the recording and matched the vibraphone part, you hooked into a groove and became part of the rhythm section. As you heard in this recording, the vibraphonist's job in a groove is usually to play chords. This is called *comping*. The part you have been playing to "Sweet" is a comping part.

Listen to the first vibraphone comping part played by itself. It is simpler than you might expect. This comping part was created to be played with the other rhythm section parts, which also sound simple, individually. When all the rhythm-section instruments play together, the groove they create sounds interesting. If all individual parts were too complex, the groove would sound muddy.

Listen to just the bass and vibraphone playing the groove. Are they playing the same rhythms or different rhythms?

4

HOOKING UP TO ROCK

The way to hook up to a groove is by learning its pulse and rhythmic feel. Then, you will be able to play a comping part that hooks up rhythmically with the rest of the band.

LISTEN 2 PLAY

Listen to the first part of "Sweet," and focus on the bass and vibraphone. Notice how the vibes' comping part on the recording uses the same rhythm as the bass. The bass line is very prominent in this tune, as it often is in rock. That is one of the reasons that the vibraphone is so hooked into the groove—it plays the same rhythms as that driving bass.

LISTEN 2 PLAY

Count along with the beat, repeating "1, 2, 3, 4" through every measure. While you count, tap your right hand along with the snare drum on beats 2 and 4. This is called the *backbeat*. A strong backbeat is one of the characteristics of rock.

Tap				
(Backbeat)		>		>
Count	1	2	3	4
(Pulse)				

LISTEN 2 PLAY

While you tap and count, tap your left hand on the quarter-note pulse, along with your counting.

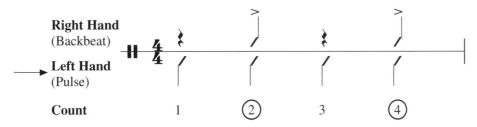

This tune has a sixteenth-note feel, so change your counting to sixteenth notes, matching the cymbals. On each beat, count evenly, "1 e + a, 2 e + a, 3 e + a, 4 e + a" ("ee and uh"). Try this first at a slower tempo, without the recording, until you get the hang of it. When you are ready, hook up with the recording.

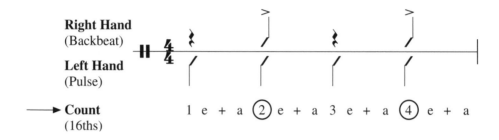

LEARNING "SWEET"

Instead of the backbeat, tap the rhythms of your comping part with your right hand. When you are ready, tap along with the recording. Hook up with the bass, which plays the same rhythm.

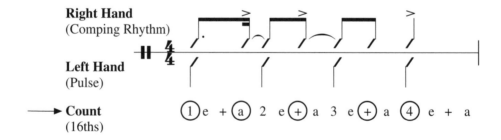

Play your first comping part along with the recording, using the written rhythms. Try to count the sixteenth notes as you play.

First Comping Part

Tap the rhythms of your second comping part, below. When you are ready, tap along with the second part to "Sweet."

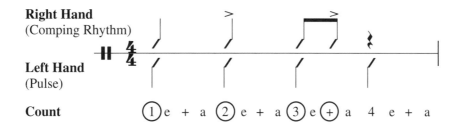

Right Hand
(Comping Rhythm)

Left Hand
(Pulse)

Count   ①e + a ②e + a ③e ⊕ a 4 e + a

Play your second comping part using the written rhythms. While you play, count the sixteenths, and hook up with the bass and bass drum.

Second Comping Part

Count   ① e + a ② e + a ③ e ⊕ a 4 e + a

LESSON 3
IMPROVISATION

Improvisation is the invention of a solo. When you improvise, you tell the story of what you think about the tune, and what it means to you. Though an improvised solo may seem spontaneous to the audience, there is a lot of preparation that comes before a musician plays it. There are two things you must know before you start improvising: when you should play, and what notes will sound good.

FORM AND ARRANGEMENT

When you are preparing to improvise on a tune, start by learning how it is organized. This will let you know when you should start improvising and where the chords change.

Listen to "Sweet," and follow the melody. After an introduction, the sax plays the song melody while the vibraphone comps. Then the vibraphone improvises a melodic solo. Finally, the sax plays the song melody again.

During the improvised solo, you can still feel the written melody. That's because the improvisation follows the same chords as the written melody. This repeating chord pattern is the same throughout the entire tune, and is called the song's *form*—its plan or structure.

A common way to show this organization is with a *chord chart*. Chord charts don't show rhythm or pitch, just measures and chord symbols. The slash marks (*/ / / /*) mean "play in time."

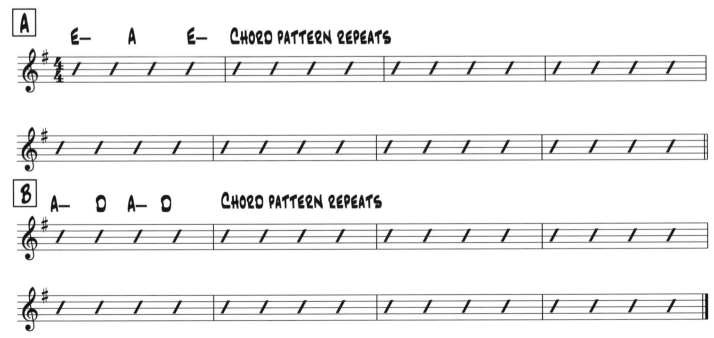

The chord chart makes it easy to see that the form of "Sweet" is sixteen measures long. It has two primary musical ideas: the first eight measures present the first idea (Idea "A"), with the **E– A E–** patterns. The second eight measures present the second idea (Idea "B"), with the **A– D A– D** patterns. This form can be described simply as "AB" or "AB form." These letters help us remember the form, freeing us from having to read while we're performing.

One complete repetition of this form is called a *chorus*. A chorus can feature the written melody, in which case it is called the *head*, or it can feature just the chord structure, supporting an improvisation. The word *chorus* is also used to mean a song section that is alternated with varying verses. In this book, however, the word "chorus" is only used to mean "once through the form."

ARRANGING "SWEET"

Your band can choose how many choruses you want to play, and create your own *arrangement* of "Sweet." The number of choruses depends on how many players will improvise when you perform the tune. On the recorded performance of "Sweet," only one player solos, playing for two choruses. Often, several members of the band will take turns playing choruses of improvised solos. A solo can be one or two choruses, or even more.

On the recording, the same basic arrangement is used for all the tunes: the head, an improvised vibraphone solo, and then the head again. There are often short introductions and endings as well. This is the arrangement for "Sweet" played on the recording:

INTRO	HEAD	VIBE SOLO: 2x	HEAD	ENDING
4 MEASURES	‖ 1 CHORUS = 16 MEASURES ‖:	1 CHORUS = 16 MEASURES :‖	1 CHORUS = 16 MEASURES ‖	2 MEASURES ‖

When you play "Sweet" with your band, you can play your own arrangement, adding extra solo choruses, different endings, or other changes.

IDEAS FOR IMPROVISING

When you improvise, some notes will sound better than others. There are many ways to find notes that will sound good. You can use the notes from the tune's melody, you can use notes from the chords, and you can use notes from scales that match the tune. Eventually, this becomes intuitive, and you can just follow your ear.

Pentatonic Scales

The vibraphone soloist on this recording of "Sweet" built much of his solo using notes from a *pentatonic scale*. Pentatonic scales are among the simplest and most versatile types of scales in all of music. All pentatonic scales have five notes. There are two common types of pentatonic scales. For "Sweet," the soloist used the *minor pentatonic scale* built on E. This scale works well here because the tune is in E minor.

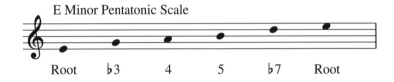

The magic of the minor pentatonic scale is that nearly any series or combination of its notes sounds musically pleasing. It is easy to improvise pentatonic *licks* (short melodic figures or phrases) that sound good.

E Pentatonic Practice

Play this pentatonic melody and chords along with "Sweet."

RANGE EXERCISE

When you learn new scales, practice them throughout the range of your instrument. A good exercise is to randomly play notes of the scale all over the instrument. Only play notes in the scale you are practicing. It might turn out like this:

LISTEN 6 PLAY

Practice randomly playing notes of the E minor pentatonic scale along with the CD. Play them in all octaves, and use your own rhythms.

CALL AND RESPONSE

Echo

Listen to each phrase, and then play it back, echoing it exactly. Each 2-bar phrase comes from the E minor pentatonic scale. Play just the melody, using one hand. Follow the form, and try to capture each phrase's rhythms. Slashes ("/") in measures marked "play" mean that you should play during those measures. Listen carefully, and hook up with the groove.

Keep practicing that track until you can echo all phrases perfectly. Then do the same thing for the phrases on this next track.

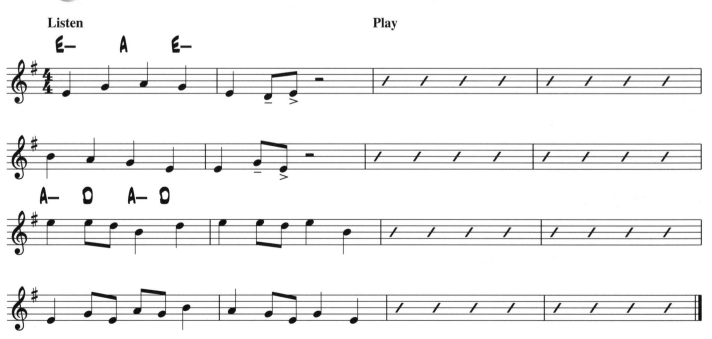

Answer

LISTEN **7,8** P L A Y

Play the same two tracks again. This time, instead of echoing the phrases exactly, answer them with your own improvised phrases. Imitate the sound and rhythmic feel of the phrases you hear, and only use notes of the E minor pentatonic scale.

Write out some of your own 2-measure phrases, like the ones you have been playing. Don't worry about perfecting your notation; just sketch out your ideas. This will help you remember them when you are improvising.

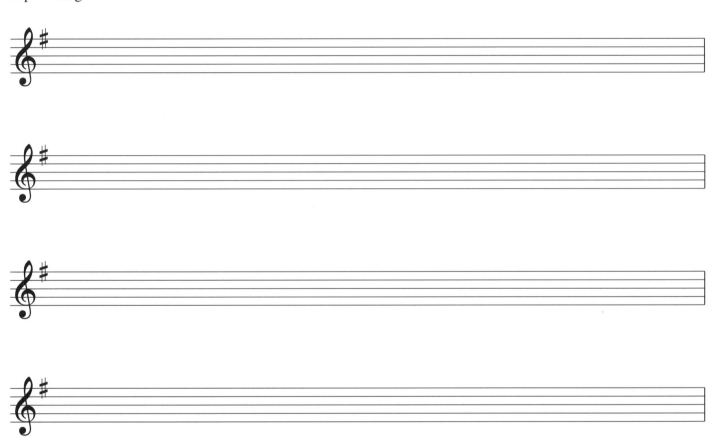

LISTEN **6** P L A Y

Create a one-chorus solo using any techniques you have learned. Memorize your solo, and practice it along with the recording.

PLAY IN A BAND TIP

When playing in a band, listen to the other players' parts and try to create a musical conversation. This makes playing much more fun, and more musical too. When you are improvising a solo, listen to what the other instruments are playing. They will suggest many ideas that you can use in your solo, and you will inspire each other.

LESSON 4
READING

Sometimes you will get a vibraphone part for the tune that shows exactly what you should play. Other times, you will get a lead sheet, giving you more freedom to create your own part. You should be able to play from either one.

VIBRAPHONE PART

On the next page is the written part to "Sweet." Above your part is a smaller staff that shows the melody and chord symbols. Some vibraphone parts show the melody, but often they do not.

INTRO	Introduction. The written part begins with an introduction, which is made up of four measures of the B section.
HARD ROCK	Style indication. This tune is hard rock, and you should play it in that style: strong beat, sixteenth-note feel, and other elements typical of that hard-edged sound.
♩ = 86	Metronome marking. This tells you how fast you should play this tune. If you have a metronome, set it to 86, and play "Sweet" at that tempo.
‖: :‖	Repeat signs. Play the music between these signs twice (or more).
A	Rehearsal letter. These are different than form letters, which you saw in lesson 3. These letters help you when you are practicing with other musicians because everyone's parts have the same letters marked at the same places.
A9	Rehearsal letter with measure number. These mark different areas within a chorus. Again, this can be helpful during rehearsals.

AFTER SOLOS, REPEAT TO ENDING

When the soloists are finished, play the head one more time, and then proceed to the measures marked "Ending."

ENDING   A final section that is added to the form. End the tune with these measures.

Play along with the recording of "Sweet," following the notated vibraphone part exactly. This part is typical of a comping part that you might create for "Sweet."

Sweet

Vibraphone Part

By Matt Marvuglio

LEAD SHEET

Lead sheets present the chords and melody, written in treble clef. Lead sheets give you more interpretive freedom than full vibraphone parts do. Notice that there is no written introduction on this lead sheet. The introduction you hear in the recording is an interpretation of the lead sheet by that band. Your band should create your own unique arrangement.

Play "Sweet" along with the recording, and follow the lead sheet, comping with the chords you learned earlier. Improvise slight variations in the comping rhythm.

SWEET

BY MATT MARVUGLIO

PLAY IN A BAND TIP

While you play, follow the lead sheet. It will help you keep your place in the form.

CHAPTER I
DAILY PRACTICE ROUTINE

TECHNIQUE/THEORY

Stickings

Sticking refers to which hand is used to play a note. An R means playing a note with your right hand, and an L means playing it with your left hand.

Alternate or *single sticking* means switching hands for each note.

Double sticking means playing two consecutive notes with the same hand.

Combination sticking is a mixture of single and double sticking.

Deciding which stickings to use is part of learning a new tune, and it can be useful to write them into your part. Different sticking patterns are useful for different types of music. For example, alternate sticking lets you play lines with a nice flow and a smooth sound. However, alternate sticking can involve a lot of arm motion. Sometimes, it is better to eliminate this by using double or combination sticking. Try this next example first with alternate stickings and then with a combination sticking. You will see how much of a difference choosing the correct sticking can make.

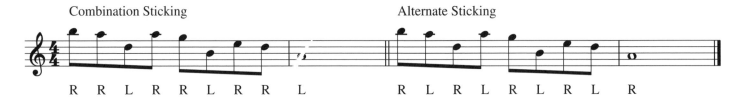

Experiment using a variety of stickings. Good technique means having the ability to use a variety of sticking combinations. Ultimately, when playing a melody or improvising, choosing the best sticking becomes automatic. Practicing sticking exercises will help you become comfortable choosing them. For example, practice scales or patterns of licks using different stickings. Here are some other exercises you can try.

Sticking Practice 1

Play this sticking exercise along with the CD. Alternate choruses using each sticking shown.

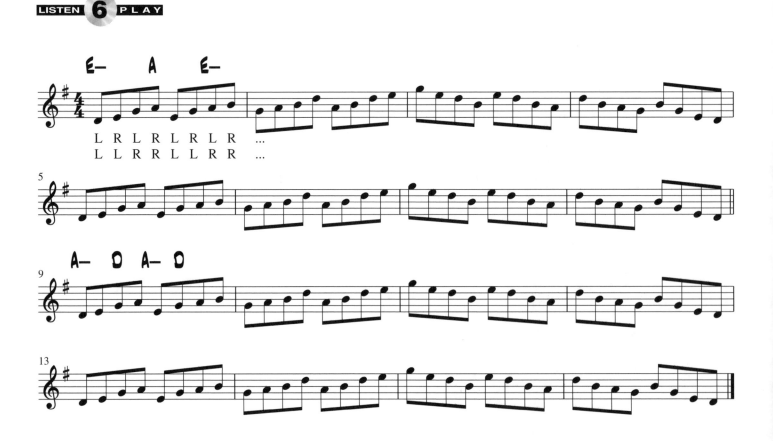

Sticking Practice 2

Use the phrase below to create a similar exercise as what you just played. Try a variety of stickings, beginning with the one shown, and stretch it over the form of "Sweet." Practice it along with the CD.

PRACTICE TIP

Practice stickings throughout the entire range of your vibraphone. When you work on exercises such as these, practice them in every register.

LEARNING THE GROOVE

This next exercise will help you create comping parts by giving you some rhythmic ideas that you can combine with your inversions. Tap the upper rhythms with your right hand, keeping a steady pulse with your left hand. Practice each group of two measures at a time. When you are ready, tap along with "Sweet."

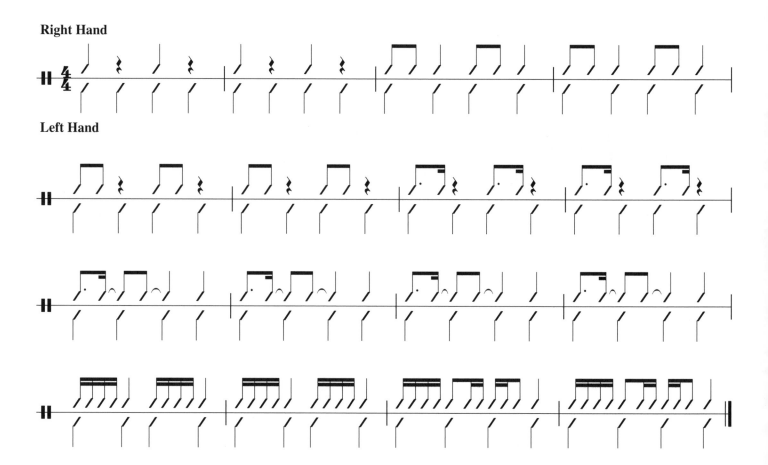

CHALLENGE

Hook up with the recording again, and tap the above rhythms in a random order of your own improvisation.

INVERSIONS

There are many ways to play a chord, as you saw in lesson 1. Pitches can be rearranged, played in different orders and octaves. When a chord tone other than the root appears as the lowest note, the chord is *inverted*. For a triad, two inversions are possible. The example below shows E minor, played in *root position* (the root is the lowest note), followed by its two inversions:

Root Position · First Inversion · Second Inversion

If the third (G) of the chord is the lowest note, then the triad is in *first inversion*. If the fifth (B) is the lowest note, it is in *second inversion*. The inversions you choose will depend on the other instruments in your band, and on the sound you want for the tune.

Here are all the inversions for the chords used in "Sweet." Practice these inversions in different octaves. Then work them into your comping patterns.

PRACTICE TIP

Think of chords and inversions as words in your musical vocabulary. When you learned to talk, you practiced using words by saying them over and over, using them in different ways. When you learn to play music, practice using chords by playing them. As you master how to put them together meaningfully, you may even use them in humorous ways. That's great! Just enjoy finding new ways to play each chord.

Practice the following chord exercise along with the recording. Become familiar with the sound of each chord and each inversion. When you change chords, there should be no hesitation between them. The move from one chord to the next should be automatic. Inversions will help you avoid unnecessary jumping, and will make comping much easier, so practice playing chords in all inversions.

Here are some comping licks for you to try. Along with the CD, play a chorus or two using each pattern throughout.

CHALLENGE

Create a comping part using the rhythms and the inversions you have been practicing.

IMPROVISATION

When you are first learning scales to use as the basis for your improvisation, be careful to avoid just playing them up and down your instrument. Here is an example of the E pentatonic scale being used in a solo, but in a way that is not very creative.

This next solo uses patterns of notes, still based on E pentatonic. The pattern makes the solo more interesting.

Playing notes close together in a scale makes your lines smooth and singable. However, sometimes using leaps (larger interval skips) in your improvisations can also help make your improvisation more interesting.

PRACTICE TIP

In this book and beyond, you will learn many techniques you can use in your solos. Remember, though, that the groove is the priority. Your goal is to play an interesting solo and to keep a strong groove.

PHRASES FOR IMPROVISING

The following phrases are typical solo ideas that you might play along with "Sweet." Practice them along with the CD. Repeat each idea (separated by double bar lines) until you can play it comfortably, then move on to the next. Be sure to hook up with the rest of the band.

SOLO PRACTICE

Practice the recorded vibraphone solo to "Sweet." When you are ready, play along with the recording. Notice that much of it is based on the E minor pentatonic scale with one additional note: B♭. We will learn more about this scale (the "blues scale") in chapter 2.

MEMORIZE

LISTEN **6** PLAY

Memorizing the licks and melodies from these exercises will help you play the tune, especially when you improvise. What you practice helps you when you perform. But performing is the best practice, so get together with other musicians and learn these tunes with your own band.

Memorize the comping part to "Sweet." Also memorize the lead sheet and a solo. The "Summary" shows everything that you need in order to play "Sweet" from a lead sheet. Memorizing it will help you memorize the tune.

PRACTICE TIP

Write out a chord chart for "Sweet" by memory. This is a good way to help memorize tunes, and you can do it anywhere or anytime. Don't worry about making it neat; just sketch out the measures and the chords, and think about solo ideas you might play over them.

SUMMARY

FORM
16-BAR AB
(1 CHORUS = 16 BARS)
A: 8 M.
B: 8 M.

ARRANGEMENT
INTRO: 4 M.
1 CHORUS MELODY
2 CHORUS SOLO
1 CHORUS MELODY
END: 2 M.

HARMONY

SCALE
E MINOR PENTATONIC

PLAY "SWEET" WITH YOUR OWN BAND!

"Do It Now" is a *blues* tune. Blues began in the late 1800s, and it has had a profound influence on American music styles, including rock, jazz, and soul. To hear more blues, listen to artists such as B.B. King, the Blues Brothers, Robben Ford, Bonnie Raitt, James Cotton, Albert King, Paul Butterfield, and vibraphonist Milt Jackson.

LESSON 5
TECHNIQUE/THEORY

Listen to "Do It Now," and then play along with the recording. Try to match the vibraphone part. In this tune, you will play three comping patterns. Listen for the rhythms.

LISTEN **9** PLAY

CHORDS: BLUES PROGRESSION

In blues tunes, such as "Do It Now," the basic chords are I, IV, and V. These chord numbers come from the major scale. Here is the F major scale and the number matching each note, or each *scale degree*.

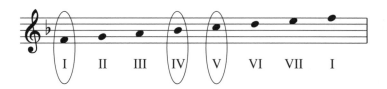

Here are the blues triads built on I, IV, and V. In the key of F, these chords are F, B♭, and C.

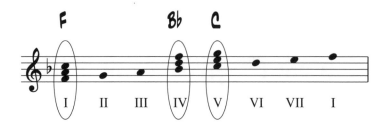

Listen to "Do It Now" and follow the bass, which plays the chord roots. Notice where the chords change. The basic blues progression uses the I, IV, and V chords in this order:

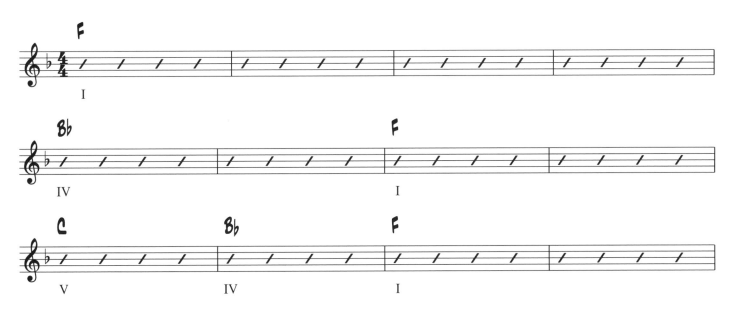

Memorize this progression. You will see it many times, in many forms of music besides blues.

BLUES COMPING PATTERNS

Notice that the vibraphone plays two different chords over each root. For example, in the first comping pattern, the chords are notated like this:

But the vibraphone part actually plays these chords:
On the recording, the vibraphone player created a part by adding the IV chord (**B♭**), and then returning to the

written I chord, **F**. Mixing in a IV chord when the song only calls for a I chord is common in blues. Choosing the right inversions makes the chord changes sound smooth. In this case, the **B♭** chord is in second inversion.

Using the chord a fourth above the written chord will make your blues vibraphone parts sound authentic. It will also add a bluesy edge to a rock or jazz tune.

CHORD SYMBOLS: SEVENTH CHORDS

Chord symbols also use numbers to describe extra pitches added to the basic triads, though they use regular numbers (1, 4, 5), rather than Roman numerals (I, IV, V). For example, you may see a chord symbol that looks like this:

The "Maj7" means that you should add the seventh scale degree of the F major scale ("Maj" stands for "Major"). When you see this symbol, play the notes of this chord:

In blues, and other styles, it is common to use chords that include the ♭7. It is often called the *dominant seventh chord*, and looks like this:

F7

This means that you should add the ♭7 of the F major scale—an E♭. You would play this:

Here are the seventh chords used in "Do It Now." They are all dominant seventh chords.

You can use seventh chords in your own comping part. For example, in this tune, instead of just returning to a simple F chord after the B♭, as you did in the first phrase, you could go to an F7, and add an E♭ to the chord:

You could do it again from the IV chord (B♭):

All these dominant seventh chord patterns are common in blues and other styles.

LESSON 6
LEARNING THE GROOVE

HOOKING UP TO A BLUES SHUFFLE

LISTEN **9** PLAY

Listen to "Do It Now." This groove has its roots in traditional r&b, gospel, and jazz. The feel is often called a *12/8 shuffle* because of the twelve eighth notes in each bar. (The drums play these on the ride cymbal or hi-hat.)

Tap your left hand on every beat, and count triplets: "1 trip-let 2 trip-let 3 trip-let 4 trip-let." The basic pulse is on the quarter note. However, each pulse also has an underlying triplet, which divides the beat into three equal parts. Tap the triplets with your right hand.

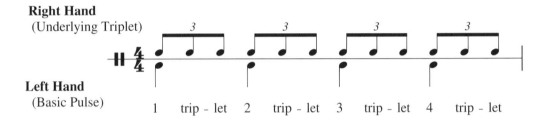

This triplet feel is part of what makes the beat a *shuffle*. While all shuffles don't include triplets on every single beat, the underlying triplet *feel* is always present.

The triplet is a fundamental aspect of all swing and shuffle beats. Understanding and feeling this concept of *subdivisions* (dividing the pulse into smaller rhythms) will help you play many kinds of grooves.

SWING EIGHTH NOTES

Eighth notes in shuffle grooves are usually played as triplets, even though they are notated as *straight* eighth notes.

Though these rhythms look different, in some styles, they are played the same. Eighth notes that are played as triplets are called *swing eighth notes*. Swing eighth notes are common in many styles of music, including blues, jazz, and swing. Sometimes, the word "swing," "swing feel," or "shuffle" appears on the lead sheet, telling you how to play eighth notes.

The notated part to "Do It Now" shows eighth notes notated like this:

Since it is a shuffle tune, they are played more like this:

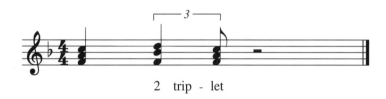

Notating triplets as straight eighths is very common in shuffle grooves.

PERFORMANCE TIP

The comping instruments play different parts during the melody and during the solo section. That's because the guitar plays the melody during the head, but adds its own comping part during the solo section, when the vibraphone solos. It also helps to shape the arrangement. If more than one instrument is comping at the same time, they often play different rhythms so that their parts fit together and do not interfere with each other. If there is a keyboardist, vibist, and guitarist in the group, sometimes it's a good idea to not have all of the players comp at the same time. They can take turns "laying out," which means not playing in order to allow the other player(s) to comp.

LESSON 7
IMPROVISATION

Listen to "Do It Now," and follow the form. Notice that the form is played twice at the head. How many times does it repeat during the improvised solo? Why does the soloist play higher in the second chorus of the improvised solo? Is the vibraphone part the same or different during the solo? Why?

FORM AND ARRANGEMENT: 12-BAR BLUES

"Do It Now" is a *12-bar blues*. As you saw in lesson 5, its form is twelve measures long.

A 12-bar blues has three 4-bar phrases. It is common for the first two phrases in the melody to be similar and the third one to be different. This form is very common in many styles of music, including jazz, rock, and funk.

"Do It Now" begins with the drum playing two beats of triplets. This is called a *pickup*—a short introduction, less than a measure long, that leads to a strong downbeat. The arrangement played on the recording is:

PICKUP	HEAD: 2x	VIBE SOLO: 2x	HEAD	ENDING
2 BEATS DRUMS	‖: 1 CHORUS = 12 MEASURES :‖	‖: 1 CHORUS = 12 MEASURES :‖	1 CHORUS = 12 MEASURES	4 MEASURES

PRACTICE TIP

When you listen to any music, figure out the arrangement. How long is the head? Is there an introduction or an ending? How many solo choruses does the band take?

IDEAS FOR IMPROVISING: BLUES SCALE

In chapter 1, you learned to improvise using the minor pentatonic scale.

Here is the F minor pentatonic scale:

The *F blues scale* has just one more note—the flat fifth scale tone (C♭ or B♮):

The blues scale is linked closely to the blues chord progression. Every note of the blues scale will sound good over every chord in the blues progression, though it has more tension than the minor pentatonic scale does. This tension makes melodies interesting, and blues scales are very popular among improvisers.

Play the F blues scale slowly over all three roots of the blues progression. Listen to how each note of this scale sounds against each of the three roots.

F Blues Scale

F Blues Scale

F Blues Scale

F Root

B♭ Root

C Root

Practice these F blues phrases along with the CD. Play each one as many times as you like, and then switch to a different phrase, choosing them in any order. Notice that any phrase will work over any chord. Try a variety of stickings for each one, and choose the sticking that suits the phrase best.

CHALLENGE

Play the F blues scale up and down, over two or three octaves. Play it with both hands. This will help you have better control over the notes of the scale while you improvise.

CALL AND RESPONSE

1. Echo each phrase, exactly as you hear it.
2. Improvise an answer to each phrase. Imitate the sound and rhythmic feel of the phrase you hear, and use notes from the F blues scale.

LISTEN **12** PLAY

Write out a few of your own ideas. Use notes from the F blues scale.

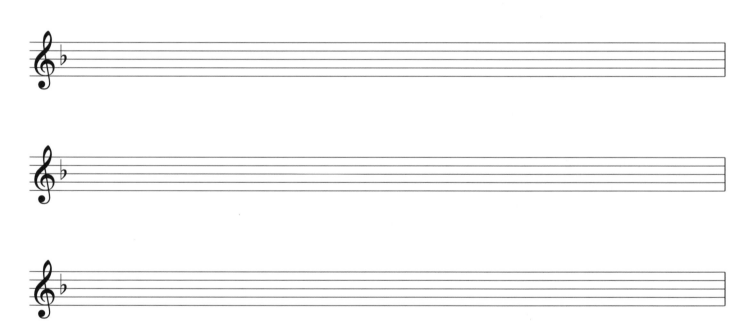

LISTEN **10** PLAY

Create a one-chorus solo using any techniques you have learned. Memorize your solo, and practice it along with the recording.

LESSON 8
READING

VIBRAPHONE PART

This *chart* (written part) uses symbols and instructions that direct you to skip around the pages. When you get the hang of these symbols, you will see that they help reduce the number of written measures and make the chart easier to read quickly, at a glance. Sometimes, these directions are called the chart's *road map*.

2 BEATS DRUMS   Pickup. Short introduction (less than a measure).

𝄋   Sign. Later, there will be a direction (D.S., or "from the sign") telling you to jump to this symbol from another location in the music.

⊕   Coda symbol. "Coda" is another word for "ending." On the last chorus, skip from the first coda symbol to the second coda symbol (at the end of the piece). This symbol may also have the words "To Coda," or other directions (such as "last time only"). Often, you will just see the coda symbol by itself.

D.S. AL ⊕   From the sign (𝄋), and take the coda. Jump back to the sign (first measure, after the pickup), and play from there. When you reach the first coda symbol, skip ahead to the next coda symbol (at the end).

AFTER SOLOS   When all solo choruses are finished, follow this direction.

𝐁   Different choruses may be marked with different letters. In this tune, the head is marked "A," and the improvisation choruses are marked "B."

SOLO   Solo chorus. Play this part when other musicians in the band improvise. When you play this tune with your own band, you might repeat this section several times, depending on how many people solo. When you solo, then obviously, you won't play this written part.

Play "Do It Now" along with the recording. Follow the vibraphone part exactly as it is written. It uses the comping patterns you have been playing throughout this chapter.

Do It Now

Vibraphone Part

By Matt Marvuglio

LEAD SHEET

Play "Do It Now" and follow the lead sheet. Play your own comping part.

LISTEN **10** PLAY

Do It Now

BY MATT MARVUGLIO

PRACTICE TIP

The more you practice reading music, the easier it becomes to play. After a while, you'll be able to look at a measure and instantly hear in your head what it should sound like. So practice reading as a regular part of your daily routine. Read through vibraphone music, piano music, flute music—anything you can find. Five or ten minutes a day is fine. Little by little, your reading skills will improve.

CHAPTER II
DAILY PRACTICE ROUTINE

STICKING PRACTICE

Practice this phrase with alternate stickings, double stickings, and combination stickings. Which way is most comfortable to you?

INVERSIONS

In chapter 1, you learned that triads have two possible inversions. Seventh chords have three possible inversions. *Third inversion* is when the seventh is in the root.

3rd Inversion

Here are the inversions for the "Do It Now" chords. Play each inversion in several octaves. Notice how their sound changes in the different registers.

The following exercise covers all the inversions of the "Do It Now" chords. Practice the chords in both right and left hands. Use some of these inversions when you create your own comping part to "Do It Now."

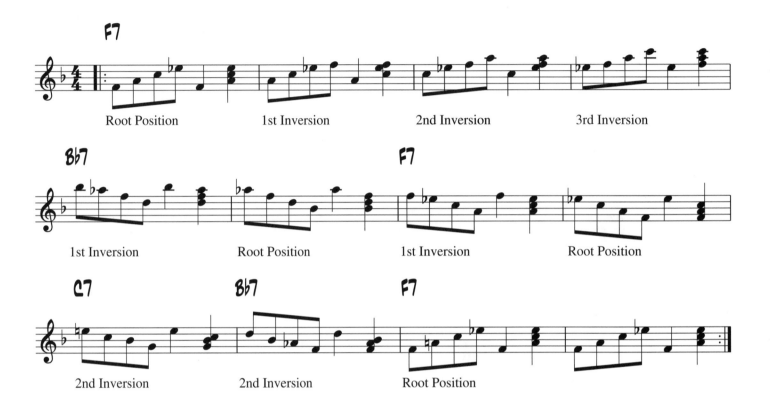

COMPING PRACTICE 1

Practice these I–IV–I patterns, which begin on different inversions. Each time, the IV chord inversion chosen is the one whose notes are closest to the I chord.

Open and Closed Position

Another option for chord voicings is close versus open position. In *close* position, the chord notes are all within an octave.

In *open* position, the chord notes are more than an octave apart. These chords still include all the notes of each chord. They are just spread out.

Depending on the tune, the other instruments in your band, and the affect you are trying to create, you may use any of these voicing options in your comping. Practice them all. Knowing a variety of voicings is helpful. For example, if you have to create a one-chord comping part based on a single chord, you can switch between several different voicings.

Try this comping part along with the CD. The comping for each chord symbol is based on two different voicings of the same chord. Notice how the simple rhythms help you lock into the groove.

COMPING PRACTICE 2

Using any of the voicing options you have learned, create a comping part using the rhythms below. Swing your eighths, and practice along with the recording.

LISTEN 10 PLAY

Comping Rhythms 1

Comping Rhythms 2

CHALLENGE

LISTEN 10 PLAY

Create a comping part to "Do It Now" using your own rhythms. Play it along with the recording.

SYNCOPATION

Syncopation means placing a note off the beat (on the "and"), rather than on the beat (on the 1, 2, 3, 4). It creates a sense of pushing the music forward, and is very common in jazz and other types of music. By placing some notes off the beat, you will keep the groove from sounding stagnant. It is very important in keeping a good time feel.

This melody has no syncopation. Every note is on the beat.

Here is the same melody, but with some added syncopation.

Syncopated   Syncopated

Syncopation Practice

This exercise uses just two notes, played with a syncopated rhythm. Begin by playing it slowly. Then gradually speed up the tempo, until you are playing it as fast as you can, without making any mistakes. Then practice it along with the CD, at the regular tempo on the recording.

Listen to "Do It Now." Where do you hear syncopation in the melody? In the bass part? In the solo? In the vibraphone part?

Music is like comedy: you need good timing. In a comedy routine, there shouldn't be any lulls, and music is the same way. The groove should flow smoothly, and the performance should have a sense of forward motion.

IMPROVISATION

Solo Phrases

LISTEN **10** PLAY

Practice these phrases along with the recording. Play each one as many times as you like, and then switch to a different phrase, choosing them in any order. Try a variety of stickings for each one, and choose the sticking that suits the phrase best. Notice the syncopations. Notice that all notes come from the F blues scale.

One way to come up with phrases for your improvisations is to start with a rhythm. As an example, here's a syncopated rhythm, played on one note only.

The next step is to plug in notes from the F blues scale, keeping the same rhythm.

SOLO RHYTHMS

What phrases can you make out of the following rhythms and notes from the F blues scale? Try several different phrases for each given rhythm, and practice them along with the recording.

LISTEN **10** PLAY

CALL AND RESPONSE

1. Echo each phrase, exactly as you hear it.
2. Improvise an answer to each phrase. Imitate the sound and rhythmic feel of the phrase you hear.
   Use the notes from the F blues scale and the solo rhythms you have been practicing.

Write out a few of your own ideas. Use notes of the F blues scale.

SOLO PRACTICE

Practice this solo to "Do It Now" along with the recording.

MEMORIZE

LISTEN **10** PLAY

Create a comping part and a solo using any techniques you have learned. Memorize your part, and then play through the tune with the recording as if you were performing it live. Keep your place in the form, and don't stop, whatever happens.

PERFORMANCE TIP

If you make a mistake or get lost, keep your composure, and pretend that everything is going fine. Listen to the other instruments, hear what chords they are playing, and find your way back into the form. You can even practice getting lost and then finding your place. Start the recording at a random point within the track, and then follow your ear.

SUMMARY

FORM
12-BAR BLUES
(1 CHORUS = 12 BARS)

ARRANGEMENT
PICKUP: 2 BEATS DRUMS
2 CHORUS MELODY
2 CHORUS SOLO
1 CHORUS MELODY
END: 4 M.

HARMONY

F7 Bb7 C7

SCALE

F BLUES

PLAY "DO IT NOW" WITH YOUR OWN BAND!

"I Just Wanna Be With You" is a *blues swing*. *Swing* is a dance-oriented, big-band style from the 1930s. The vibraphone first entered the popular music spotlight in this style of music when it was featured on a recording of Lionel Hampton performing with Louis Armstrong. To hear more swing, listen to artists such as Count Basie, Benny Goodman, the Squirrel Nut Zippers, Diana Krall, Branford Marsalis, Kevin Eubanks, Joanne Brackeen, Cherry Poppin' Daddies, Big Bad Voodoo Daddy, and vibraphonists Lionel Hampton, Red Norvo, and Bobby Hutcherson.

LESSON 9
TECHNIQUE/THEORY

Listen to "I Just Wanna Be With You," and then play along with the recording. Try to match the vibraphone part. In this tune, you will play three comping patterns. Notice that the first pattern returns after the third pattern.

LISTEN 15 PLAY

First Comping Pattern	**Second Comping Pattern**	**Third Comping Pattern**
	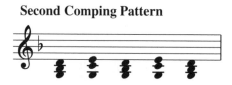	

BLUES SWING COMPING PATTERNS

"I Just Wanna Be With You" is also a blues tune. The chords follow the same blues pattern, using the I, IV, and V chords, as "Do It Now." The difference is that this tune is based on minor chords.

This tune also uses the same I–IV–I chord comping patterns as "Do It Now." In these comping patterns, the I chords are all minor triads, but the IVs are all major. Minor and major chords in the same pattern gives minor-blues tunes a unique sound.

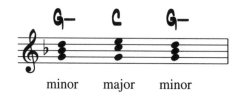

INVERSIONS FOR COMPING PATTERNS

In the first comping pattern, there are two chords: D minor and G major. Here are the inversions for both chords.

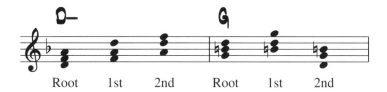

In the comping pattern, the I chord (**D–**) is in first inversion. The IV chord (**G**) is in root position.

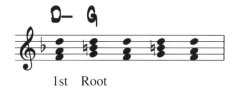

We use different inversions for the two chords so that the comping pattern sounds smooth. If both chords were in root position, it would sound choppy.

The way that one chord moves to another is called *voice leading*. Using the right inversions leads to smoother voice leading and better comping parts. Smooth voice leading helps the vibraphone part blend into the groove. In the actual comping pattern, notice that the top note "D" appears in both chords and stays in the same position. The other notes all move by only a step. We say that such a part "has smooth voice leading" or simply "is voice led." When you move to a new chord, generally you should move each voice as little as possible, unless you are trying to get a disjointed effect.

PEDALING

The pedal allows notes to ring together. When you play melody, you may find that the pedal gives your lines a fuller, more musical sound.

Generally, the right foot is used for pedaling. Your feet should stay in the same position, regardless of whether you are playing on the low end or the high end of the instrument. Your right heel should stay in contact with the ground. Pedal markings are often indicated using brackets. Hold the pedal down through all notes connected by the bracket.

Pedal
Down

Pedal
Up

Pedaling works best for melodies that outline a chord or for longer notes. It helps chords sound fuller. If the melody outlines a chord, or is comprised of all intervals of a third or larger, you can hold the pedal through all the notes. When comping, the pedal helps keep a smooth, sustained sound. Just release the pedal when the harmony changes.

When the melody is stepwise or includes many fast notes, avoid using the pedal, as it can blur the melody line. As a rule, it is better to use less pedal than too much pedal.

Try the melody to "I Just Wanna Be With You" with three different pedalings.

1. No pedal.
2. Pedal all the way through.
3. Pedaling as shown.

Which way sounds best?

The pedal can become a crucial part of your sound. It opens up many options for phrasing and articulation. You can even use it as a source for improvisation ideas. Try to alternate stepwise motion with larger leaps.

LESSON 10
LEARNING THE GROOVE

HOOKING UP TO SWING

Listen to "I Just Wanna Be With You," and focus on the cymbals. This tune is a shuffle, like "Do It Now." There is a triplet feel under each beat. The main difference is that in this tune, the middle triplet of each beat is left out. This is common in swing.

Shuffle
("Do It Now")

Swing Shuffle
("I Just Wanna...")

This syncopated "push-pull" feel is basic to jazz and r&b. Sometimes this feel is called a "double shuffle" because the drummer plays the same rhythm with both hands. In swing, the bass player usually plays a "walking" quarter-note bass line.

Notice how the sax interprets the ♫ of the melody. The eighth notes are uneven, or "bounced." Try to sing or play along with the sax. This will help you get into the swing feel.

LEARNING "I JUST WANNA BE WITH YOU"

Listen carefully to the rhythms from the melody indicated below. These same rhythms are picked up by the vibraphone comping part. After listening to the melody, play along with the comping rhythm. Imitate the rhythmic feel that the sax uses in rhythms 1 and 2.

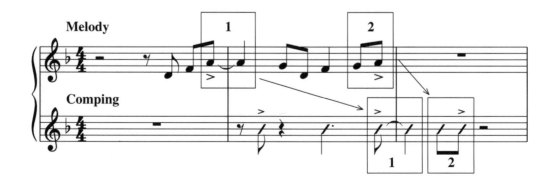

Let's break down the comping rhythm into two rhythms. Tap quarter notes with your foot. With your hand, tap this rhythm.

The first measure of the comping rhythm is the same except that the first attack is *delayed*.

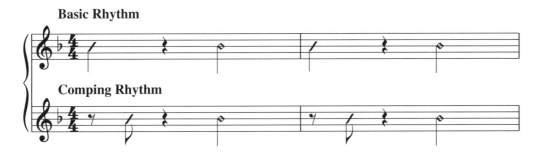

Now, look at the second measure of the comping part. Notice that the third attack is *anticipated*—played before the beat. Tap quarter notes with your foot, and the comping rhythm with your hand.

One more rhythm will complete this comping pattern. Start with the comping rhythm above. Then, anticipate the first attack.

When you are comfortable playing these rhythms, you will be ready to find this tune's groove.

LESSON 11
IMPROVISATION

FORM AND ARRANGEMENT

Listen to "I Just Wanna Be With You," and follow the form. This tune is another 12-bar blues. The form of each chorus is twelve measures long and divided into three phrases, just like "Do It Now."

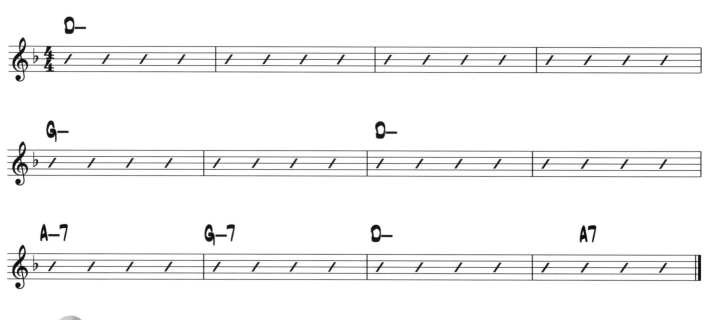

LISTEN 15 PLAY

Listen to "I Just Wanna Be With You," and follow the arrangement. Is there an introduction or ending? What part of the form did these added sections come from?

This is the arrangement used on the recording:

INTRO	HEAD: 2x	VIBE SOLO: 2x	HEAD	ENDING
4 Measures	‖: 1 Chorus = 12 Measures :‖	‖: 1 Chorus = 12 Measures :‖	1 Chorus = 12 Measures ‖	8 Measures ‖

The intro and ending come from the form's last four measures. On the recording, the band chose to play the ending twice. This kind of repeated ending is called a *tag ending*.

PERFORMANCE TIP

Sometimes, a band may decide to "tag a tune" (play a tag ending) several times, building energy with each repetition. If things are going well and everyone is in the mood, a band may even make an ending longer than the rest of the tune. This is a place where people really let loose and have fun playing. When you listen to music, pay attention to what a band is doing at the end of a tune.

Scale: D Blues

Though the soloist on the recording favors the D minor pentatonic scale, the D *blues* scale will also work well for this tune. It has one additional note—the A♭:

Play the D blues scale with your right hand, up and down within the octave.

MOTIVES

A *motive* is a short melodic idea. Here is a 3-note motive based on notes from the D blues scale.

You can base your improvisations on motives, repeating them exactly or making slight alterations. Here is a longer melody that was created by repeating this motive, but beginning it on different notes of the scale. Repeating motives is an effective way to retain the listener's interest, giving the melody a sense of cohesion and structure.

This repeated motive forms a pattern. There are many ways to do this. In this next example, the first two motives are identical, and the third one is different.

Here is an example of a motive that can be used throughout a solo. Repeating an idea like this makes it memorable for the listener. It can be used throughout all of a form or for just a few measures. Practice this example along with the recording.

CALL AND RESPONSE

1. Echo each phrase, exactly as you hear it.
2. Improvise an answer to each phrase. Imitate the sound and rhythmic feel of the phrase you hear, and use the notes from the D blues scale. Also try thinking of them as motives, and playing them back beginning on a different note.

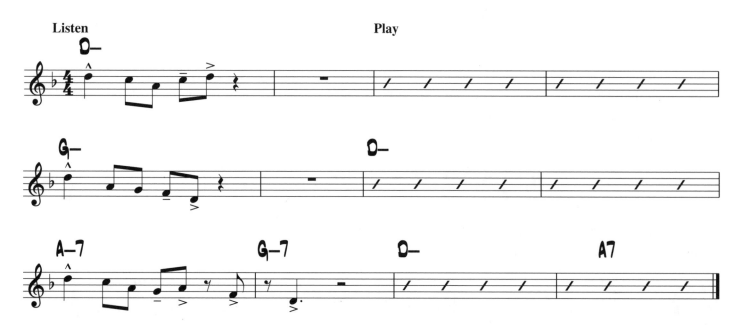

Write out a few of your own ideas. Use the D blues scale.

Create a one-chorus solo using any techniques you have learned. Part of it should be based on repeating a motive. Memorize your solo, and practice it along with the recording.

LESSON 12
READING

VIBRAPHONE PART

Play "I Just Wanna Be With You" while reading from the written vibraphone part. Play it as written.

 Two-measure repeat. Repeat the previously-notated two measures.

LISTEN **16** PLAY

I Just Wanna Be With You
Vibraphone Part

By Matt Marvuglio

LEAD SHEET

Play "I Just Wanna Be With You" from the lead sheet, using your own comping part. There are two new notation items here:

$(\xi \; \bar{\downarrow} \;)$ Break your regular comping rhythm when you see this (last measure) and play this rhythm instead.

INTRO/ENDING Though this lead sheet doesn't show an introduction or ending, you and your band can create your own. The intro can be just drums, as you saw in "Do It Now," or it can come from the last line of the tune, as it does on the recording. Tag the ending at least three times, repeating the last four measures of the written part.

LISTEN **16** PLAY

I Just Wanna Be With You

BY MATT MARVUGLIO

CHAPTER III
DAILY PRACTICE ROUTINE

BLUES SCALE PRACTICE

Practice this blues scale exercise along with the recording.

STICKING PRACTICE

Practice this sticking exercise along with the recording.

Choose your own stickings for this next exercise, and write them into the part. Then practice it along with the recording. If you find a better sticking than what you originally wrote, use that one instead.

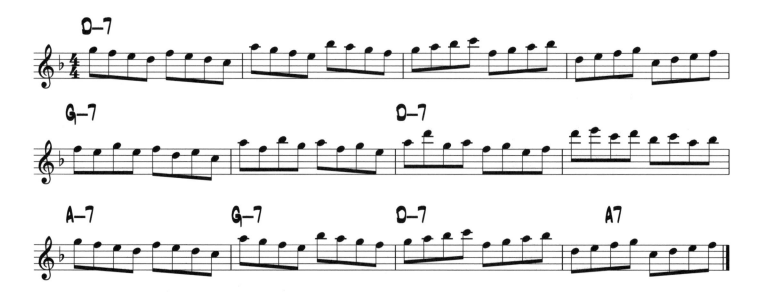

INVERSION PRACTICE

Practice this inversion exercise along with the recording.

Voicing Practice

Here are some open voicings for the chords used in this tune. Build a comping part using some of these chords, alternating them with close voicings. Practice your part along with the recording.

COMPING PRACTICE

Using any of the voicing options you have learned, create a comping part using the rhythms below. Swing your eighths, and practice it along with the recording.

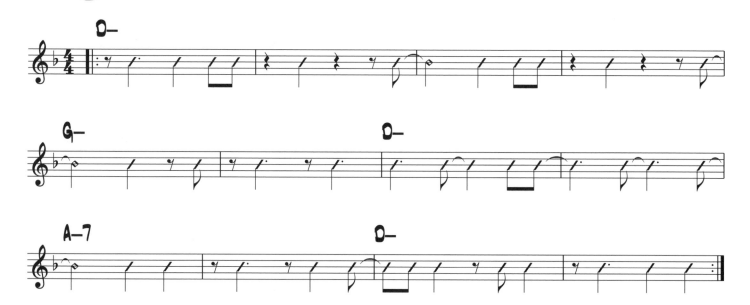

BLUES LICKS

Practice these blues licks along with the recording. Play them in any order you wish.

MELODY/COMPING PRACTICE

Practice playing melody against a comping part, first by yourself, and then with the recording.

CHALLENGE

While you play chords in your left hand, improvise with your right hand using the D blues scale.

DRONE EFFECTS

Try these blues licks.

1. Practice the D minor blues scale with an added upper note. Think of the lower note as the melody and the upper note as a *drone* (sustained) harmony. Practice slowly, up and down the scale, until it feels natural.

2. Now, practice dividing the scale into triplets, adding the drone on the first of each triplet group.

CHALLENGE

LISTEN **16** PLAY

Create a one-chorus solo that uses the drone effect. Practice it along with the recording.

SOLO PRACTICE

Practice this solo to "I Just Wanna Be With You" along with the recording. Notice its use of motives.

MEMORIZE

Create your own comping part and improvised solo to "I Just Wanna Be With You." Practice it along with the recording, and memorize it.

SUMMARY

PLAY "I JUST WANNA BE WITH YOU" WITH YOUR OWN BAND!

"Leave Me Alone" is a *funk* tune. Funk has its roots in New Orleans street music. It started in the 1960s and is a combination of rock, r&b, Motown, jazz, and blues. Funk has also influenced many rap artists. To hear more funk, listen to artists such as James Brown, Tower of Power, Kool and the Gang, the Yellowjackets, Chaka Khan, Tina Turner, the Red Hot Chili Peppers, and vibraphonists Mike Mainieri and Roy Ayers.

LESSON 13
TECHNIQUE/THEORY

Listen to "Leave Me Alone," and then play along with the recording. Try to match the vibraphone part. In this tune, you will play three comping patterns:

LISTEN **19** PLAY

First Comping Pattern **Second Comping Pattern** **Third Comping Pattern**

DOUBLE STOPS

A *double stop* is two notes played at the same time. When you play chords, you are playing double stops. They can also be included as part of melody parts. The most common double stops are octaves, thirds, and sixths, though any interval can be effective in the right place.

Octaves **Sixths** **Thirds**

Double stops have a bigger sound than single notes, and they can add depth to your line. Often, the interval of the stop will change from note to note. This example shows a melody first played as single notes and then played as double stops, with a repeated high G.

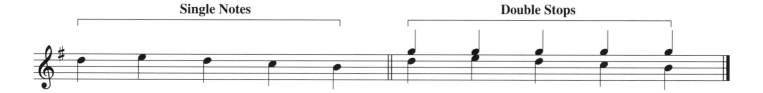

Double stops are common in blues styles, and many other styles too. Here is a typical blues lick that uses a double stop. Keyboard and guitar parts often include them too. Again, a top note is repeated. This repeated note is most often the root or fifth of the blues scale being used, but any note from the blues scale can be effective. Here, the root of the G blues scale repeats.

LESSON 14
LEARNING THE GROOVE

HOOKING UP TO FUNK

LISTEN **19** PLAY

Listen to "Leave Me Alone." This funk groove has its roots in New Orleans street music—funky march music played on marching instruments (snare drums, bass drums, and so on) still found in the Mardi Gras parades each spring. Many New Orleans artists were important to the development of funk.

Funk rhythms are played with less of a swing feel than blues. There is an underlying sixteenth-note feel, similar to rock. Beats 2 and 4 are often accented, usually by the snare drum.

SYNCOPATION

In the last chapter, you learned to play syncopated eighth notes. In funk, syncopations are often on sixteenth notes. "Leave Me Alone" has a syncopated sixteenth note at the end of the second beat. This note interrupts the regular pulse.

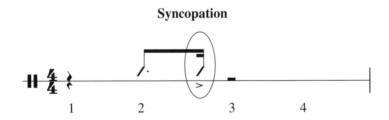

To get the right feel, start by clapping the second note on beat 3.

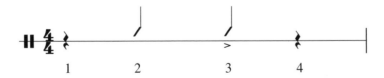

Next, clap the the second note a sixteenth sooner. It comes right before beat 3. This type of syncopation is often called an *anticipation* because it "anticipates" the beat.

Play your comping part using the written rhythms. Feel the anticipated rhythm.

LESSON 15
IMPROVISATION

FORM AND ARRANGEMENT

Listen to "Leave Me Alone," and follow the form. This funk tune follows the 12-bar blues form.

LISTEN **19** PLAY

On the recording, the arrangement begins with a 4-measure introduction, featuring the rhythm section playing the groove.

INTRO	HEAD: 2x	VIBE SOLO: 2x	HEAD
4 Measures	‖: 1 Chorus = 12 Measures :‖	‖: 1 Chorus = 12 Measures :‖	‖: 1 Chorus = 12 Measures :‖

IDEAS FOR IMPROVISING

Scale: G Blues

The G blues scale will work well for this tune:

Dynamics

Dynamics are how loud or soft your notes are. A melody can be made more dramatic by using dynamics. Sometimes, you will see dynamics written into a part. Other times, none will be written, so you will have to choose which dynamics to play. Of course, when you improvise, you will have to create your own dynamics, but it can be helpful to notate them if you write out your solos. Here are some of the common symbols used for dynamics.

Symbol	Name	Meaning
p	piano	soft
f	forte	loud
mp	mezzo piano	medium soft
mf	mezzo forte	medium loud
<	crescendo	get louder
>	diminuendo	get softer

Play this melody as written, with no dynamics.

Play it again, but use the dynamics shown. Notice how it becomes more interesting and dramatic.

Next, try the following two phrases. They are the same notes, but with different dynamics. Notice how different they sound.

Play this phrase using a variety of dynamics. Try several ways to play it.

CONTRAST

Having contrasting dynamics will make your playing more interesting. Other kinds of contrast have the same effect. For example, notes of different durations can help bring a solo alive.

You can also use the pedal to add contrast. Keep some phrases dry, but let others ring.

Playing some phrases straight while syncopating others also adds contrast.

Phrase length can also be a way to find contrast. Notice how some phrases are short and some are longer.

These and other kinds of contrast all help make your soloing more interesting. When music is all fast and loud, it gets boring, after a while. Even though it might be impressive technically, the listener's attention will wander. But if fast, loud passages are played in the context of slower, softer ones, they will all be much more effective.

Listen to the recorded solo to "Leave Me Alone." Notice where the soloist uses contrast in his playing.

LISTEN **19** PLAY

CALL AND RESPONSE

1. Echo each phrase, exactly as you hear it.
2. Improvise an answer to each phrase. Imitate the sound and rhythmic feel of the phrase you hear, and use the notes from the G blues scale. Try to play phrases that contrast with the ones you hear.

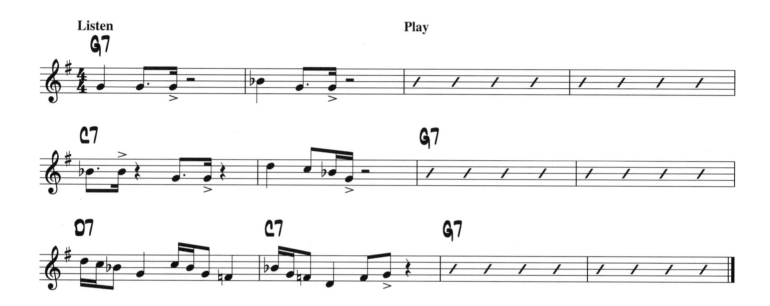

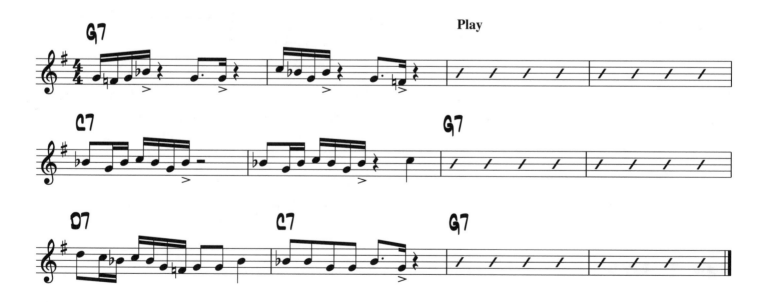

Write out a few of your own ideas.

LISTEN 22 PLAY

Create a one-chorus solo using any techniques you have learned. Memorize your solo, and practice it along with the recording.

LESSON 16
READING

VIBRAPHONE PART

 A bar with a number over it means that you should rest for that number of measures. The introduction here is just bass and drums, so you can sit out. But count along, so you are ready to come in on the fifth measure.

Play "Leave Me Alone" along with the recording, using the written vibraphone part.

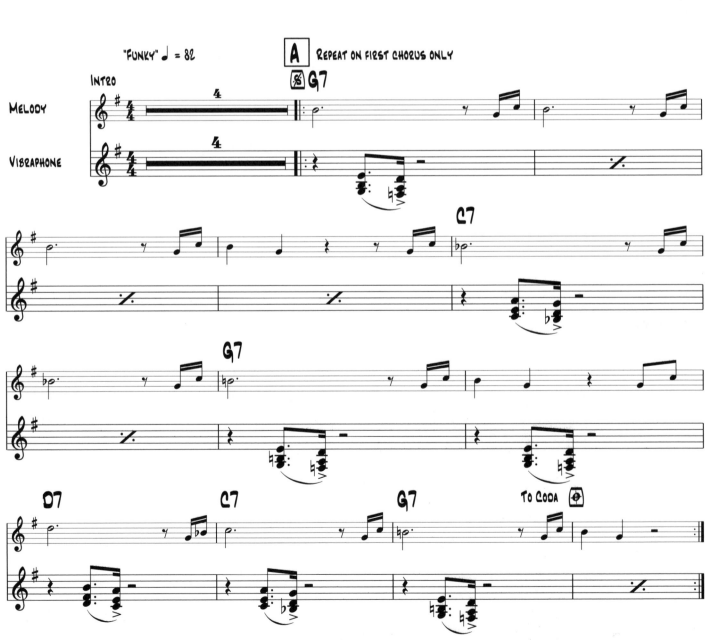

LEAVE ME ALONE
VIBRAPHONE PART

By Matt Marvuglio

PRACTICE TIP

Memorizing your notes makes it easier to follow arrangement directions, such as "D.S. AL ⊕."

LEAD SHEET

Play "Leave Me Alone" along with the recording, and follow the lead sheet. Play your own comping part.

LEAVE ME ALONE

BY MATT MARVUGLIO

CHAPTER IV
DAILY PRACTICE ROUTINE

INVERSION PRACTICE

Here are all the inversions for the chords used in "Leave Me Alone."

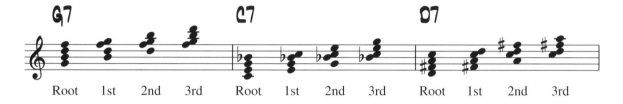

Practice this inversion exercise along with the recording.

Try these comping parts to "Leave Me Alone." The first uses a common funk voicing technique: moving the chord down by a whole step. It is most common on dominant 7 chords.

This second comping part moves the chords chromatically.

HOOKING UP

Practice hooking up with the funk groove's sixteenth-note feel. Tap the quarter-note pulse with your left hand and the upper rhythms with your right hand. Repeat each rhythm until you can play it easily.

LISTEN **22** PLAY

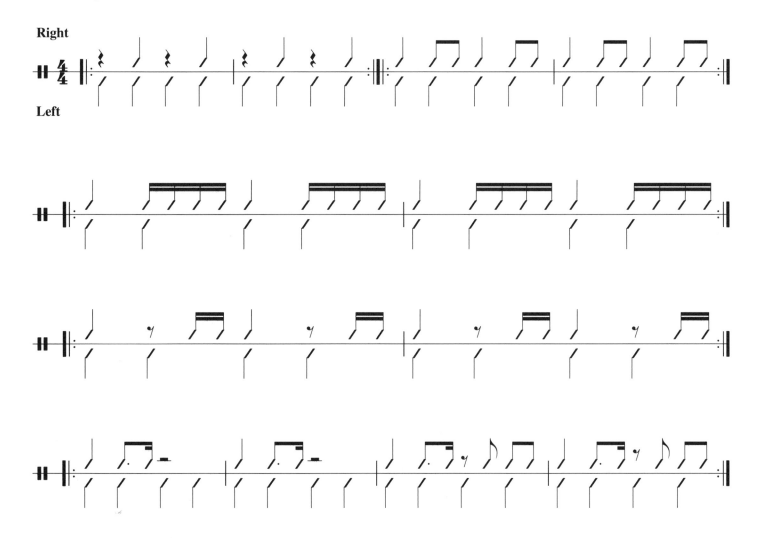

CHALLENGE

Play this exercise again, and count "1 e + a, 2 e + a, 3 e + a, 4 e + a" as you tap quarter notes with your left hand. For an added challenge, play and count along with the recording. Try switching hands.

This comping part uses some funk voicings and rhythms. Notice the sixteenth-note syncopations. Practice it along with the recording.

COMPING RHYTHMS

Use these rhythms with chord voicings of your choice to create comping parts for "Leave Me Alone." Practice them along with the recording.

> ### PRACTICE TIP
> Before playing a new rhythm, tap or clap it first, away from your instrument.

CALL AND RESPONSE

1. Echo each phrase, exactly as you hear it.
2. Improvise an answer to each phrase. Imitate the sound and rhythmic feel of the phrase you hear, and use the notes from the G blues scale.

Licks

Practice these licks. Notice the dynamics, syncopations, double stops, and other techniques we have studied in this chapter.

Add your own dynamics to these licks, and then practice them.

Practice these double-stop lines.

Practice these lines. They have syncopations and dynamic contrast.

Write out a few of your own ideas.

LISTEN **22** PLAY

Create a one-chorus solo using any techniques you have learned. Memorize your solo, and practice it along with the recording.

SOLO PRACTICE

Practice this solo to "Leave Me Alone" along with the recording. Write in your own dynamics.

MEMORIZE

Create your own comping part and improvised solo to "Leave Me Alone." Practice it along with the recording, and memorize it.

Summary

Play "Leave Me Alone" with your own band!

"Affordable" is another funk tune, but it is lighter, with more of a feeling of open space. This style is popular with smooth-jazz artists, such as in the late 1960s, when Gary Burton revolutionized vibraphone technique and possibilities by playing with four mallets and in a more contemporary style. His use of dampening and four mallets took the instrument into new areas of vibe playing. To hear more light funk, listen to artists such as David Sanborn, Earl Klugh, Walter Beasley, the Rippingtons, Dave Grusin, Kenny G, Bob James, Anita Baker, and vibraphonists Gary Burton, Joe Locke, and Dave Samuels.

LESSON 17
TECHNIQUE/THEORY

Listen to "Affordable," and then play along with the recording. Try to match the vibraphone. This tune has two parts.

LISTEN 25 PLAY

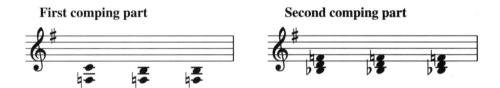

CHORDS: ADDING COLOR TO SEVENTH CHORDS

Vibists sometimes add notes to seventh chords to make a comping part more interesting. This is similar to what you saw in the I-IV-I blues pattern—adding a IV chord when only a I chord is indicated on the lead sheet. Two common additions to seventh chords are the 4 and the 9.

Added 4

The first part of "Affordable" is based on the **G7** chord.

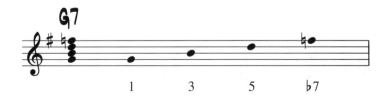

The first comping part uses a common comping pattern for seventh chords: moving to the standard **G7** chord from a **G7** chord with a 4 (C) instead of a 3 (B). This kind of chord is called a *sus4*.

Here is a **G7sus4**:

Play the first part to "Affordable," and notice the **G7sus4** moving to a **G7**.

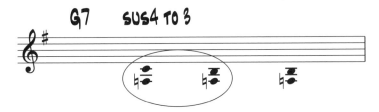

If the lead sheet had "**G7sus4**," instead of "**G7**," the chord would not need to move to the **G7**. The second comping part in "Affordable" is based on a written **C7sus4**. Since sus4 is specified, the part "suspends" the 4 above C (F) over the whole section.

Added 9

It is also common to add the 9 to a comping part. The second comping pattern of "Affordable" is a good example. The written chord symbol is a **C7sus4** chord.

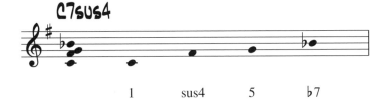

The vibraphonist on the recording added a 9 (D) to his comping part to give it more color.

Notice that the upper three notes form a B♭ major triad. Another way to describe this chord is with the symbol B♭/C. This means a B♭ chord with the note C in the bass. You may see it written either as B♭/C or as C7sus4, but the notes are the same.

Try adding a sus4 or 9 to your own comping parts. It is a good way to add color to your chords.

LESSON 18
LEARNING THE GROOVE

HOOKING UP TO LIGHT FUNK

LISTEN 25 PLAY

Listen to "Affordable." This groove is built around eighth notes, with some syncopated sixteenths in the B section. Notice that the band hooks up with the bass drum.

To learn this feel, practice counting sixteenths, leaving out the middle two sixteenths of each beat. Count out loud, along with a metronome or click track on the quarter-note pulse.

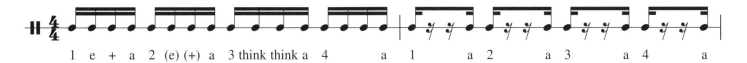

1   e   +   a   2   (e) (+) a   3 think think a   4   a   1   a   2   a   3   a   4   a

The melody of "Affordable" is mostly made up of long, sustained notes. Listening to the rest of the rhythm section and counting will help you keep your place.

In these exercises, tap the quarter-note pulse with your left hand and eighth notes with your right hand. Remember that the eighth notes are played straight, not with a swing feel. This is a slow tempo, so be careful not to rush. Let's start with the second measure of the comping rhythm and compare it to an unsyncopated rhythm:

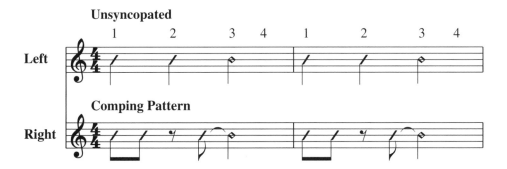

Notice that the second and third attacks are anticipated one-half beat early. Tap quarter notes with your left hand and this comping rhythm with your right hand until you can do it comfortably.

The rhythm of the first measure of the comping pattern is similar except that there is one more attack. Compare this rhythm to four straight quarter notes.

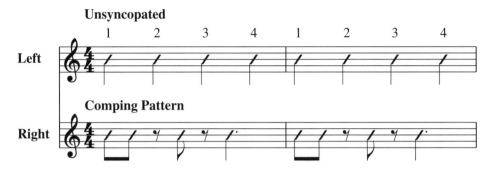

Notice that the second, third, and fourth attacks are all anticipated. Again, tap quarter notes with your left hand and the comping rhythm with your right hand until you can do it comfortably.

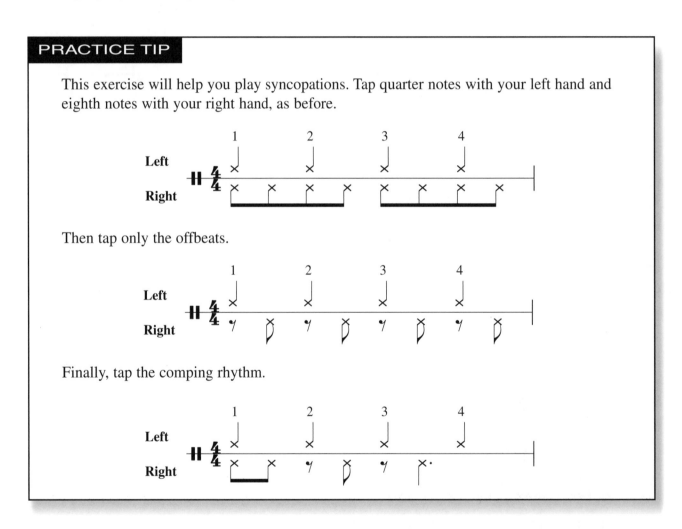

In the recorded comping part to "Affordable," the A section patterns are syncopated and the B section are regular and straight. This creates contrast between the two sections and makes the whole tune sound more interesting.

LESSON 19
IMPROVISATION

FORM AND ARRANGEMENT

Listen to "Affordable" and follow the saxophone melody over the 16-bar form.

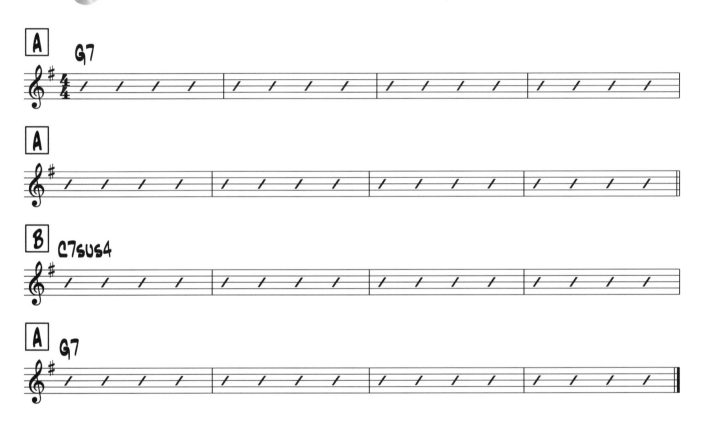

As you have already seen from practicing the comping patterns, there are two primary musical ideas in this tune. The sax plays contrasting melodies over them. Idea A is very sparse. It lasts for eight measures, with two phrases of sax melody. Idea B is in a more regular rhythm. It lasts for four measures. Then Idea A returns for four measures. This form can be described simply as "AABA."

PRACTICE TIP

Imagine the melody as you play your comping part. This will help you keep your place—particularly during improvised solos, when nobody plays the melody. Although the form of this tune is simple, it is easy to get lost. The 4-measure return of Idea A at the end of the form may be confused with the eight measures of Idea A that begin the new chorus. Altogether, there are twelve measures of this idea, so keep careful count.

Listen to the whole tune. Sing the melody while the saxophone plays the solo, and keep your place in the form. What is the arrangement on the recording? Is there an introduction or ending? Check your answer against the summary at the end of this chapter.

IDEAS FOR IMPROVISING

Grace Notes

When playing a melody, whether it is the song melody or an improvisation, you can embellish one or more notes by adding a *grace note*—a short note immediately before the written note, which is called the *primary* or *target*. Grace notes are notated as small eighth notes, often with slashes through them (♪). They are generally played using alternate sticking.

The most common grace notes are a half step above or below the primary.

You can also have several grace notes in a row. These will usually go up the chromatic scale to the primary.

Grace notes are common in melodies that have blue notes. They are common in other instruments too, such as sax or guitar.

A grace note's function is to embellish the melody, so make sure that the primary melody note is clearly heard. It should be a slight alteration, giving just a little variety to the line. Avoid using the pedal on grace notes; it would make the grace note cover over the primary note.

When you learn a melody, first practice it without grace notes, so that you have a clear idea about how the melody sounds.

Then add the grace notes. Remember, they are nuances. Keep the primary melody clear.

Practice these two phrases as written. Then add your own grace notes. Remember, keep the primary melody clear.

Scales: G Pentatonic

The G major pentatonic scale will work well for the A section of this tune:

The G minor pentatonic scale will work well for the B section of this tune:

CALL AND RESPONSE

1. Echo each phrase, exactly as you hear it.
2. Improvise an answer to each phrase. Imitate the sound and rhythmic feel of the phrase you hear, and use the notes from the G pentatonic scales. Use some grace notes in your answer, but be sure that the primary note is clear.

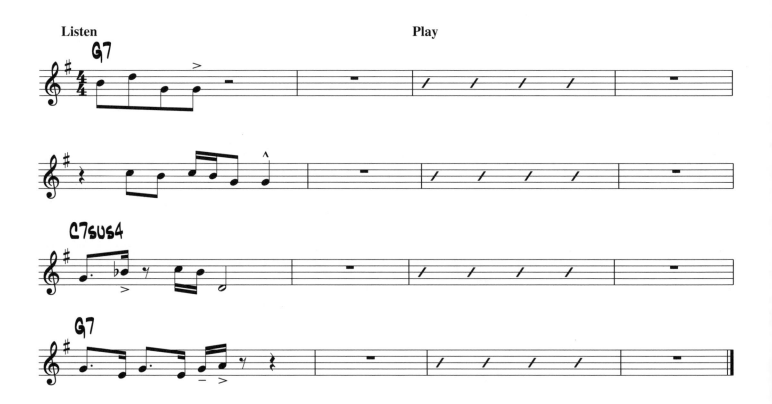

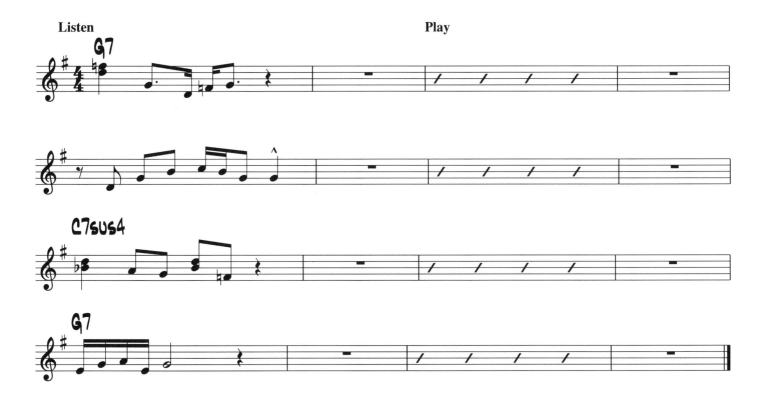

Write out a few of your own ideas. Use the G pentatonic scales.

Create a one-chorus solo using any techniques you have learned. Memorize your solo, and practice it along with the recording.

VIBRAPHONE PART

Play "Affordable" along with the recording. Use the written vibraphone part. Notice the use of bass clef. This reduces the need for ledger lines.

LEAD SHEET

Play "Affordable" along with the recording, and follow the lead sheet. Create your own comping part.

LISTEN 28 PLAY

AFFORDABLE

By Matt Marvuglio

"Light Funk" ♩ = 118

CHAPTER V
DAILY PRACTICE ROUTINE

TECHNIQUE/THEORY: INVERSION PRACTICE

Practice the inversions of the **G7**, **G7sus4**, and **C7sus4** chords:

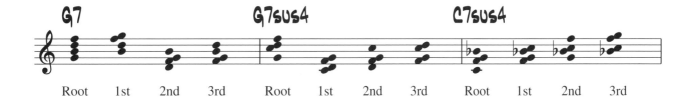

Practice the inversions of the chords used in "Affordable."

MIXOLYDIAN SCALES

Another scale you can use to improvise on this tune is the Mixolydian scale. Use the G Mixolydian scale during the "A" sections of "Affordable," over the **G7** chords:

Use the C Mixolydian scale during the "B" section, over the **C7sus4** chords.

Play the following exercise, and listen carefully to the sound and character of each note. Also try it starting on different steps of the Mixolydian scales.

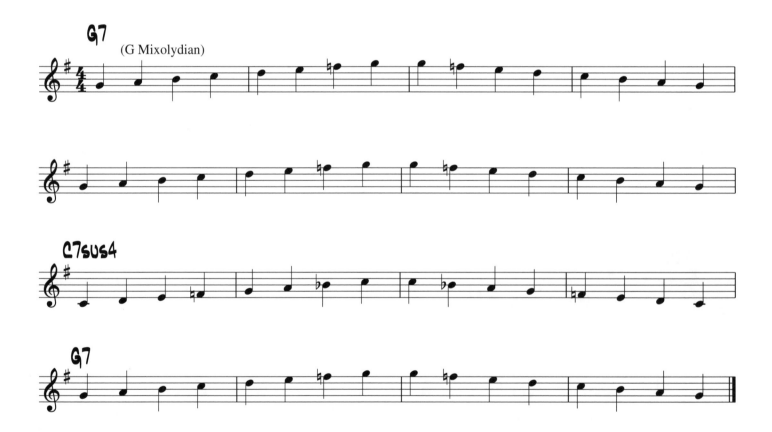

HARMONIZING THE MELODY

Using the notes of G Mixolydian, complete a second inversion triad under each scale note, using only scale notes. This is a common technique vibraphone players use to harmonize melodies in funk and other styles.

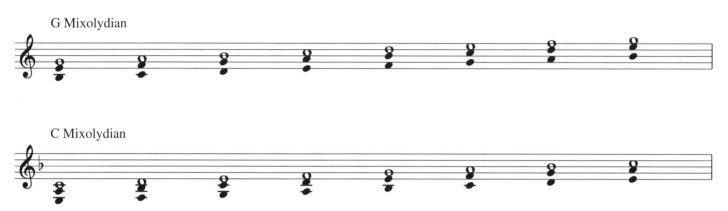

Practice playing the melody of "Affordable," harmonizing each melody note using the above technique. Play the scale roots with your left hand.

COMPING RHYTHMS

Use these rhythms with chord voicings of your choice to create comping parts for "Affordable." Practice them along with the recording.

LICK PRACTICE

These licks use grace notes, double stops, syncopations, and other musical ideas we have been discussing. They are typical of the kind of phrases that you should create for your own solo. Practice them until you can play each one easily, and then play them along with the recording, in any order.

ENSEMBLE ETIQUETTE

When you play in a band, you are a member of a team. You are making the sound of the whole band together.

If you are comping, your job is to make the soloist sound good. Try to make his job easier by supporting and listening. Remember, the soloist is in the driver's seat. Your playing should not distract from the solo. Keep your comping simple, and avoid being too busy or too loud. If there is a guitar or keyboard in the band as well, remember that you don't all have to comp all the time. It might be better for just one of you to comp, and the other two to sit out. Take turns. It's a great way to add some variety to your band's performance.

If you are soloing, take about the same number of choruses as the other people who are soloing. If they play one or two choruses, you should play one or two choruses, not ten or fifteen.

Think about the performance as a whole group, not just your own playing. By performing a lot and by listening to a lot of music, your skills as a performer will improve. When you watch a group of live musicians, notice how they listen and respond to each other. Notice how they support each other.

A common problem with bands is volume. One player might start out playing too loud. Then someone else will turn up their volume to match them. And then someone else will turn up, and so on, until everyone is playing loud. Consequently, there will be no sense of dynamic balance between the players. Try to avoid this. Make sure your volume isn't overpowering. If someone else is too loud, it might be because they can't hear themselves due to amp placement or other factors. Try to correct the problem, rather than just turning up your own volume.

Remember, your primary goal is to make the overall group performance the best that it can be.

SOLO PRACTICE

Practice this solo to "Affordable" along with the recording.

MEMORIZE

LISTEN **28** P L A Y

Create your own comping part and improvised solo to "Affordable." Practice it along with the recording, and memorize it.

SUMMARY

FORM
16-BAR AABA
(1 CHORUS = 16 BARS)
A: 4 M.
B: 4 M.

ARRANGEMENT
INTRO: 8 M.
1 CHORUS MELODY
1 CHORUS SOLO
1 CHORUS MELODY

HARMONY

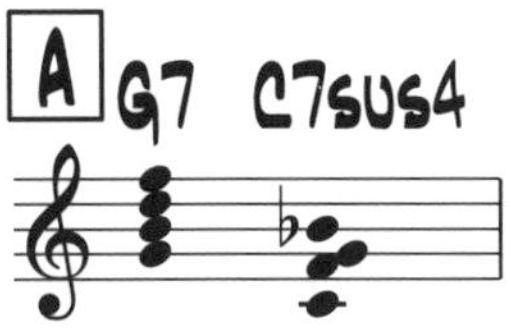

A G7 C7SUS4

SCALE

B G MAJOR PENTATONIC   G MINOR PENTATONIC

PLAY "AFFORDABLE" WITH YOUR OWN BAND!

"Don't Look Down" is a *hard rock* tune. Hard rock first appeared in the late 1960s. It has characteristic heavy bass, long, drawn-out chords, and amplified instruments. To hear more hard rock, listen to guitar-oriented bands, such as Aerosmith, Metallica, Powerman 5000, the Allman Brothers Band, Rob Zombie, Godsmack, 311, Stone Temple Pilots, Black Crowes, Steve Vai, Smashing Pumpkins, and vibraphonist Ruth Underwood (Frank Zappa).

LESSON 21
TECHNIQUE/THEORY

Listen to "Don't Look Down," and then play along with the recording. Try to match the vibraphone part. This tune has two parts.

LISTEN **29** PLAY

First comping part   Second comping part

PAD COMPING

The chords are long and sustained in this tune. This way of playing chords is called *pad comping*. The vibraphone is perfect for pad comping since the chords can sustain for long periods.

Pad comping works well especially when the other instruments are playing busier parts. "Don't Look Down" has a busy bass line and rock drum beat, as well as an active melody. The pad comping part holds it all together:

LESSON 22
LEARNING THE GROOVE

HOOKING UP TO HARD ROCK

LISTEN **29** PLAY

Listen to "Don't Look Down." This tune has a standard rock/metal groove. It is a heavy feel, with very simple drum and bass parts. These parts must be simple because they are intended to be played in large arenas, where echoes would make busier parts sound muddy. It's a case of "less is more."

Eighth notes are played straight, not with a swing feel. The bass drum plays on beats 1 and 3, which is typical of rock drum beats.

Listen to a few choruses of "Don't Look Down." Find the pulse and clap on the backbeat, along with the snare drum.

$$
\overset{}{1} \qquad \overset{>}{2} \qquad \overset{}{3} \qquad \overset{>}{4}
$$

Tap the quarter-note pulse with your foot, clap the backbeat, and count the sixteenths. When you are ready, do this along with the recording.

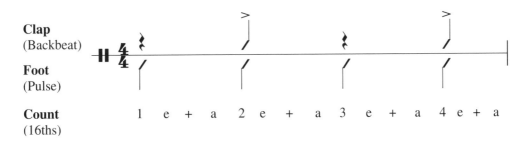

LEARNING "DON'T LOOK DOWN"

LISTEN **30** PLAY

"Don't Look Down" has two different parts with two different rhythmic feels. In the first part, the vibraphone plays the pad comping chords. Since there is just one attack on the downbeat of each measure, these are easy to play.

Listen to the first part of "Don't Look Down." Feel the sixteenth-note subdivision even when you play simple parts like this, especially if you plan to improvise a solo, where you might decide to use faster rhythms.

The second part has a syncopation. Clap the comping rhythms to the second part of "Don't Look Down." Accent the syncopated note.

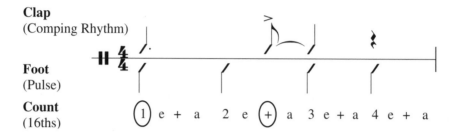

Play the second written comping part. While you play, count the sixteenths and hook up with the groove.

LESSON 23
IMPROVISATION

FORM AND ARRANGEMENT

Listen to the recording, and try to figure out the form and arrangement by ear. How long does each section of the form last? Is there an introduction or ending? For how many measures or beats does each chord last? Write down as much information as you can. Check your answers against the vibraphone part in the next lesson.

This tune has a 20-bar AB form. Part A has an active riff that builds a lot of tension. It lasts for sixteen measures. Part B is less active than the first part. It lasts for four measures. There is a 4-measure introduction at the beginning of the tune that comes from the B section.

LISTEN **29** PLAY

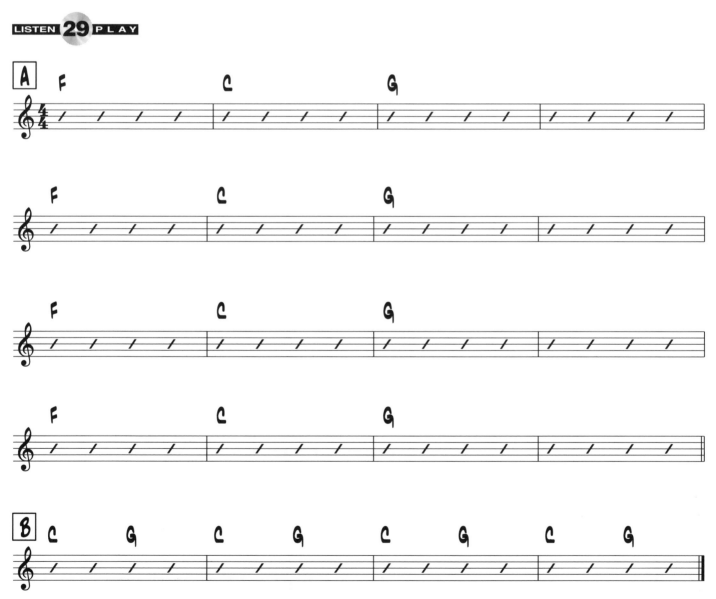

What is the arrangement on the recording? Figure it out by ear, and then check your answer against the summary at the end of this chapter.

IDEAS FOR IMPROVISING: G PENTATONIC SCALES

Scales

The G major pentatonic scale will work well for the A section of this tune:

The G minor pentatonic scale will work well for the B section of this tune:

Chord Tone Melodies

In addition to the scales, you can also build your melodies using notes of the chords. The ability to outline the chords in your improvisations is important. A good solo supports the song's harmony. Though many solos will use notes from both the scales and chords, you can also play melodies that come from the chords alone. Play this melodic phrase, and notice how it outlines the chords of "Don't Look Down."

With a chord-tone solo, avoid sounding like you are just playing up and down the arpeggios, as in this next example. The above phrase sounds much more musical than this one does.

(Avoid)

Another rut to avoid is always beginning a new chord on the root.

(Avoid)

Skips help make a chord-tone melody sound less like an arpeggio. This is sometimes called playing with "angularity."

CALL AND RESPONSE

1. Echo each phrase, exactly as you hear it.
2. Improvise an answer to each phrase. Imitate the sound and rhythmic feel of the phrase you hear, and use the notes from the G pentatonic scales. Also try to answer using melodies in octaves.

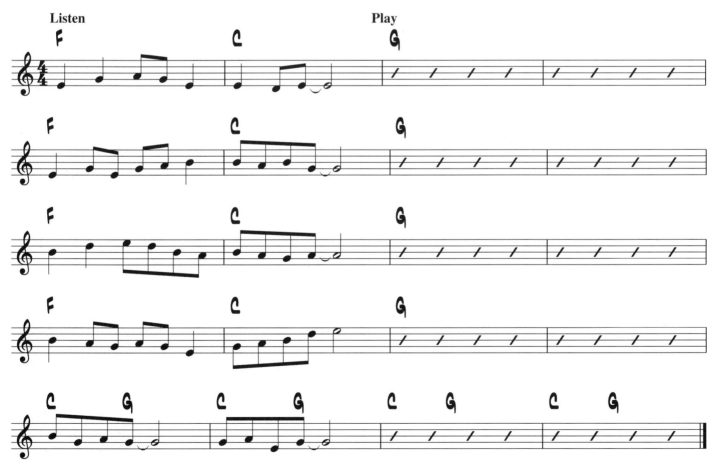

Listen

Play

Write out a few of your own ideas.

LISTEN **34** P L A Y

Create a one-chorus solo using any techniques you have learned. Memorize your solo, and practice it along with the recording.

LESSON 24
READING

VIBRAPHONE PART

Play "Don't Look Down" along with the recording. Use the written vibraphone part.

 First and second ending markings. The first time you play these measures, play the *first ending*—the measures under the number 1. Then return to the begin-repeat sign (‖:). The second time, skip the first ending and play the *second ending*—the measures under the number 2. Then, continue through the rest of the form.

DON'T LOOK DOWN

VIBRAPHONE PART

BY MATT MARVUGLIO

LEAD SHEET

This lead sheet shows the bass/guitar riff (see the ending), which you can double with low notes in your left hand.

LISTEN **34** PLAY

DON'T LOOK DOWN

BY MATT MARVUGLIO

PERFORMANCE TIP

When you play from a lead sheet, use it to help you keep your place. Even when you keep repeating the same comping patterns, follow along with the melody and chords as they are played by other instruments.

CHAPTER VI
DAILY PRACTICE ROUTINE

INVERSIONS

These are the inversions to the chords in "Don't Look Down." Practice them in all octaves.

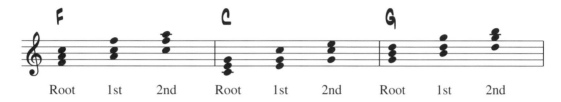

Practice this inversion exercise with the recording.

COMPING RHYTHMS

Practice comping to "Don't Look Down" using each of these rhythmic phrases. Create your own variations, and practice along with the recording. Hook up with the groove.

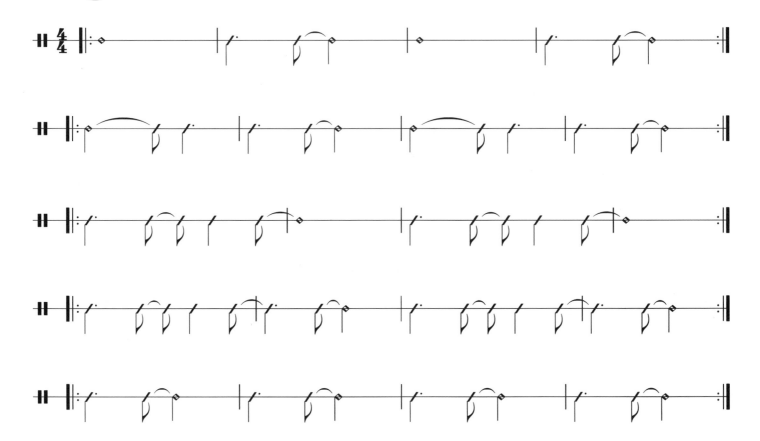

IMPROVISATION

Octaves

Playing a melody in octaves make it sound fuller. In the swing era (1940s to 1950s), when sound systems were more primitive, instruments such as vibraphone and piano had trouble being heard over the saxophones, trombones, and drums. Playing octaves was a way to be louder. This was particularly important when those instruments were soloing.

Try this melody, first playing just the bottom notes and then playing the octaves. Notice how much fuller the octaves sound.

To gain speed and accuracy playing octaves, practice playing scales and arpeggios in octaves. Use your wrists as much as possible, and try to minimize your forearm motion. Practice along with the recording.

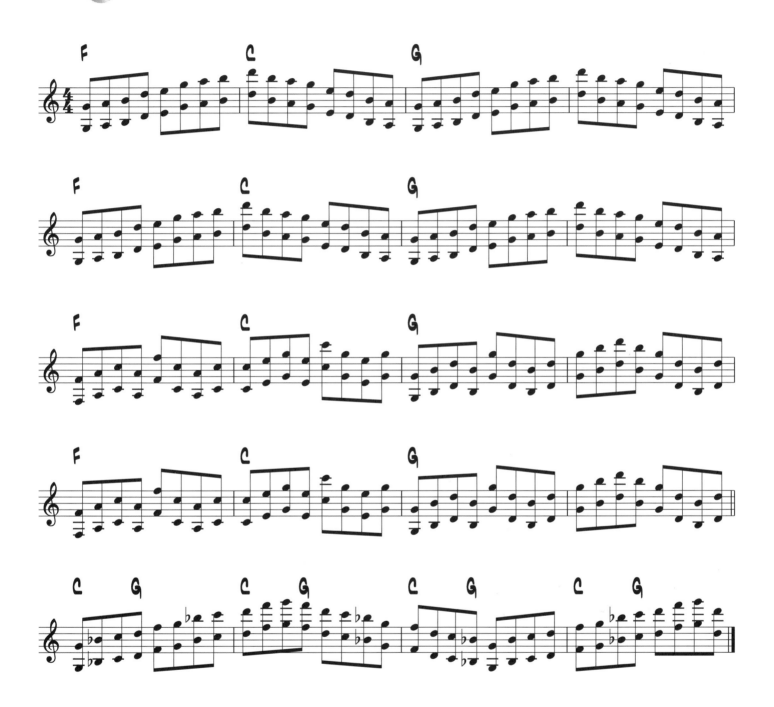

Practicing chromatic scale exercises in octaves will also help you build agility and control.

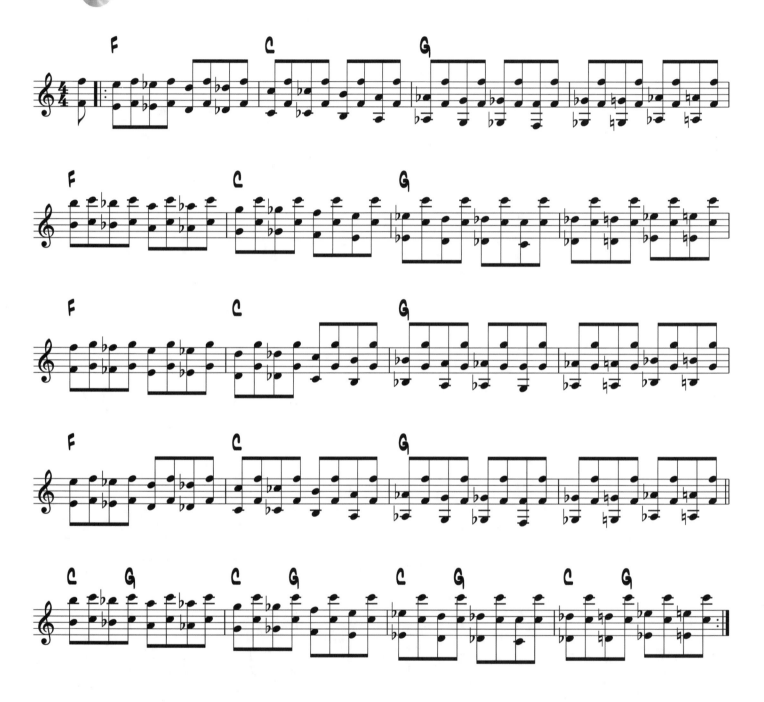

SOLO RHYTHMS

The following rhythms are typical of what you might use in your hard rock solos. Take each rhythm, one at a time, and plug in notes from the G pentatonic scales or a different chord. Practice each rhythm over several measures, or even a whole chorus. Then mix up the rhythms, using them in any order, repeating them or changing rhythms each measure. Tap them out away from your instrument before you play them.

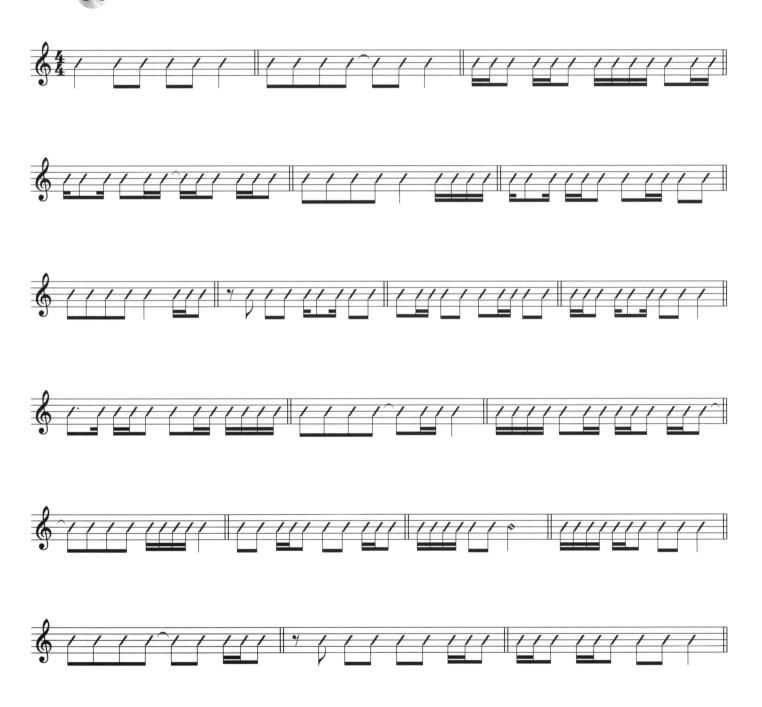

MELODY/COMPING PRACTICE

Comp in your left hand while you improvise with your right hand. Keep your left hand comping part softer than your right hand melody. Play several choruses, and try a variety of approaches. Use the G major and minor pentatonic scales, the licks you studied in this chapter, and licks that you improvise while you are playing.

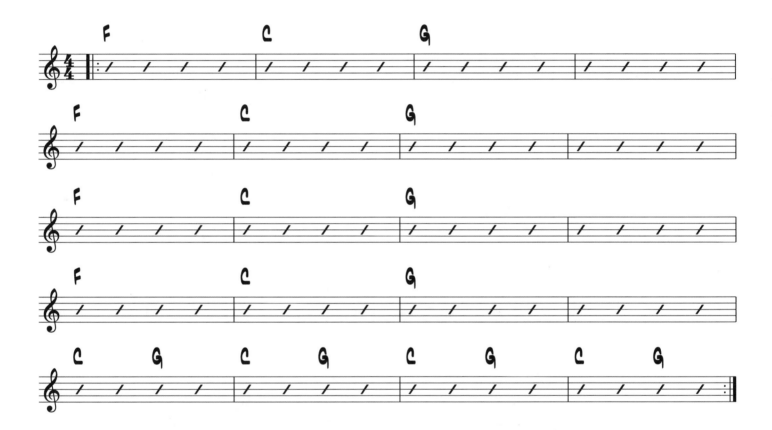

SOLO PRACTICE

Practice this solo to "Don't Look Down" along with the recording.

MEMORIZE

LISTEN **34** PLAY

Create your own comping part and improvised solo to "Don't Look Down." Practice it along with the recording, and memorize it.

SUMMARY

FORM	ARRANGEMENT	HARMONY	SCALE
20-BAR AB FORM	INTRO: 4 M.		
(1 CHORUS = 20 BARS)	1 CHORUS MELODY	F C G	G MAJOR PENTATONIC G MINOR PENTATONIC
A: 16 M.	1 CHORUS SOLO		
B: 4 M.	1 CHORUS MELODY		
	END: 2 M.		

PLAY "DON'T LOOK DOWN" WITH YOUR OWN BAND!

"Take Your Time" is a *bossa nova* tune. Bossa nova began in Brazil, combining American jazz and an Afro-Brazilian form of dance music called *samba*. To hear more bossa nova, listen to Stan Getz (with Gary Burton), Antonio Carlos Jobim, Eliane Elias, Astrud Gilberto, Flora Purim, Dave Valentine, Spyro Gyra, and vibraphonists Cal Tjader and Victor Mendoza.

LESSON 25
TECHNIQUE/THEORY

Listen to "Take Your Time," and then play along with the recording. Try to match the vibraphone part. Notice that all three phrases share the same rhythm. In this tune, you will play three comping patterns.

LISTEN **35** PLAY

First Comping Pattern

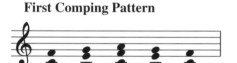

Second Comping Pattern

Third Comping Pattern

PASSING CHORDS

The comping patterns in this tune each use a *passing chord*. This chord connects two inversions of the comping pattern's primary chord.

The first pattern is based on the **D–7** chord (the root D is played by the bass). The triads use different inversions. The passing chord (circled) in this example is the II chord of **D–**, **E–7**.

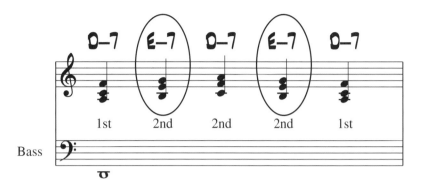

This is the same technique you saw in the blues chapters, when you used the IV chord. Passing chords help make comping patterns more melodic. Since they are generally not held for a very long time, they don't change the harmonic sound of the part.

Play the other two comping patterns of this tune, and notice the use of passing chords.

LESSON 26
LEARNING THE GROOVE

HOOKING UP TO BOSSA NOVA

Listen to "Take Your Time." This tune is a bossa nova, a style of music that originated in Brazil. Throughout the tune, a 2-bar rhythmic pattern repeats. This repeating pattern is an essential part of bossa nova. The drum plays it on a rim-click.

Repeating rhythmic structures are at the heart of much African-based music, including Afro-Caribbean and most South and Latin American styles.

Find the pulse, and tap quarter notes with your left hand and eighth notes with your right hand. Remember that the eighth notes are played straight, not swing style.

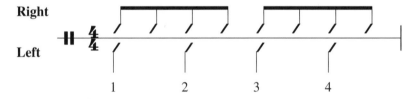

Next, accent the eighth notes as shown. This will be the essential part of your comping rhythm.

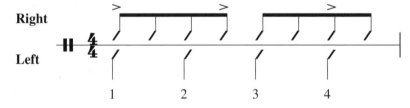

Now, tap only the accented notes and you have the rhythm!

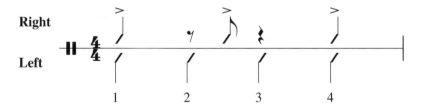

Finally, tap the entire comping rhythm.

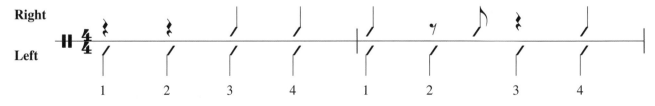

LESSON 27
IMPROVISATION

Listen to "Take Your Time," and try to figure out the form and arrangement by ear. Then continue with this chapter.

FORM AND ARRANGEMENT

This tune follows a 16-bar AB form. Each phrase of the melody lasts for eight measures.

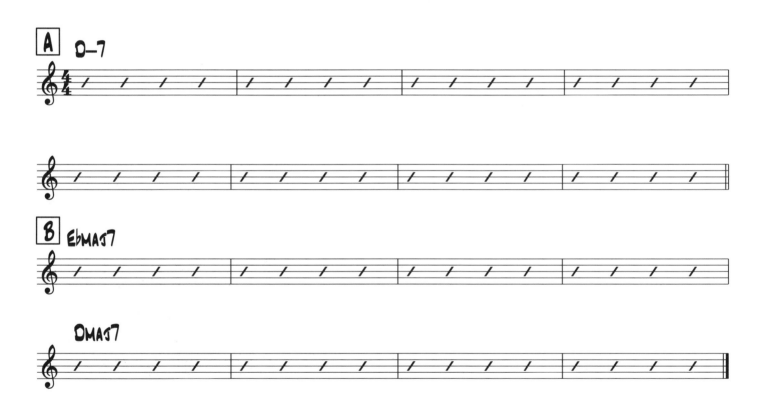

What is the arrangement on the recording? Figure it out by ear, and then check your answer against the summary at the end of this chapter.

IDEAS FOR IMPROVISING: SCALES

In this tune, try using two different scales when you improvise.

For the **D–7** and **E♭MAJ7** chords, use the D minor pentatonic scale.

For the last four measures, on the **DMAJ7** chord, use the D major pentatonic scale.

CALL AND RESPONSE

1. Echo each phrase, exactly as you hear it.
2. Improvise an answer to each phrase. Imitate the sound and rhythmic feel of the lick you hear, and use the notes from the D pentatonic scales.

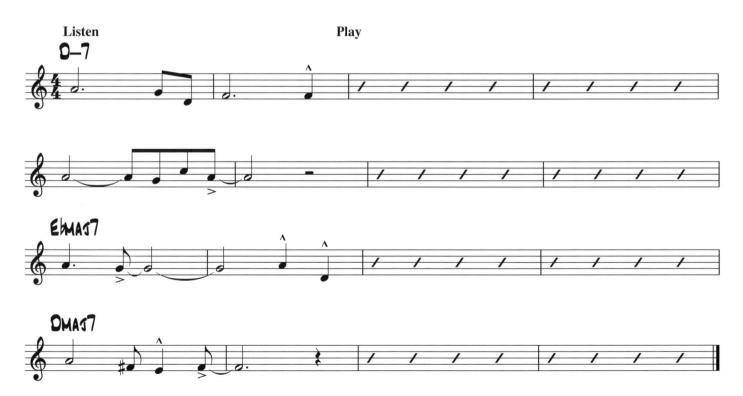

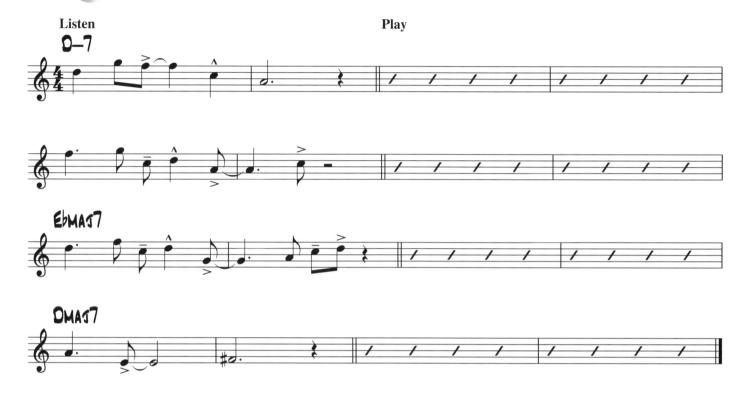

Listen   **Play**

Write out some of your own ideas. Use notes from the D pentatonic scales.

Create a one-chorus solo using any techniques you have learned. Memorize your solo, and practice it along with the recording.

VIBRAPHONE PART

Play "Take Your Time" and use the written comping part.

TAKE YOUR TIME

Vibraphone Part

By Matt Marvuglio

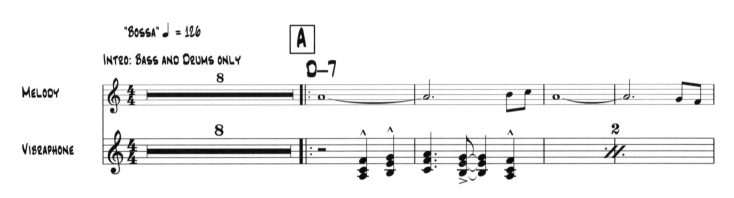

LEAD SHEET

Play "Take Your Time" and follow the lead sheet. Create your own comping part, and practice it with the recording.

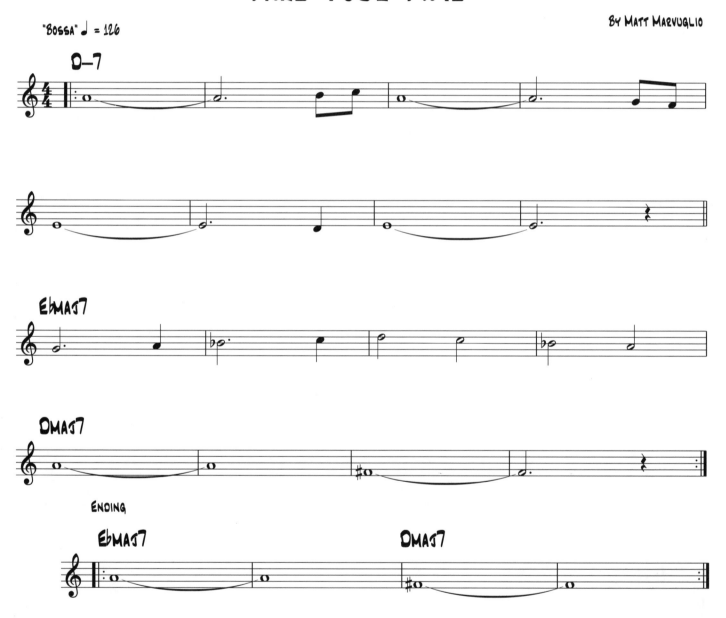

CHAPTER VII
DAILY PRACTICE ROUTINE

TECHNIQUE

Sticking Practice

Practicing chromatic patterns will help you develop your technique. Throughout each exercise, use the stickings shown, and continue the pattern throughout the range of your instrument.

Chromatic Exercise 1

Chromatic Exercise 2

Chromatic Exercise 3

INVERSION PRACTICE

These are the inversions to the chords in "Take Your Time." Practice them in all octaves.

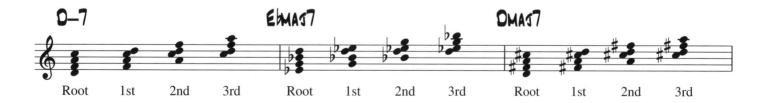

Practice this inversion exercise. As an added challenge, create your own left-hand accompaniment to the right-hand inversion exercise. Use your own rhythms for either part.

Practice these comping variations, which begin on different inversions of the "Take Your Time" chords.

COMPING RHYTHMS

The following rhythms are typical of what you might use for bossa nova comping. Notice that they are each two measures long. Use these rhythms with chord voicings of your choice to create comping parts for "Take Your Time." Practice them along with the recording.

IMPROVISATION

There are many kinds of scales that you will eventually work into your improvising. These three scales are good resources for your improvisations. Throughout your career, you will learn many others, and explore them in increasing depth.

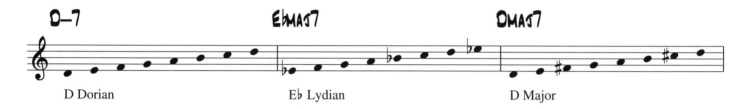

Play the root/seventh in your left hand while you play the scales with your right hand. Notice how different the scales sound, even though each begins on a "D." (When you are improvising, you can begin and end scales on any note.)

Scale Practice

You can use these three scales for improvisation ideas. Here is an example of a melody that uses the D Dorian scale.

Notice how different it looks and sounds when the notes are adjusted to fit the **EbMAJ7** chord, using **Eb** Lydian:

And different still on **DMAJ7**, using D major:

Try writing your own melodic phrase and adjusting the notes as necessary to fit the other chords.

SOLO PRACTICE

Practice this solo to "Take Your Time" along with the recording.

LISTEN **38** PLAY

MEMORIZE

LISTEN **38** PLAY

Create your own comping part and improvised solo to "Take Your Time." Practice it along with the recording, and memorize it.

SUMMARY

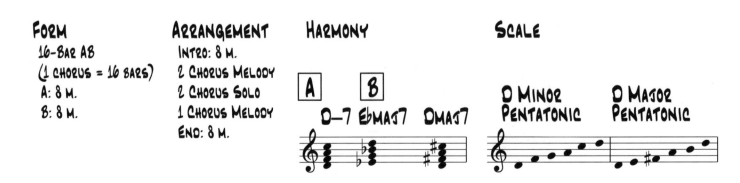

PLAY "TAKE YOUR TIME" WITH YOUR OWN BAND!

"Stop It" is a blues/jazz tune in which *stop time* accents the melody, like a question and answer. Stop time is very common in blues, jazz, and other styles. It was also popular among the bebop musicians, when vibraphonist Milt Jackson became known for taking bebop lines as played by Charlie Parker, Bud Powell, and Dizzy Gillespie, and applying them to his instrument. To hear more stop time blues, listen to artists such as Miles Davis, John Coltrane, Jim Hall, Sarah Vaughn, Bill Evans, Ella Fitzgerald, Louis Armstrong, Abbie Lincoln, Dizzy Gillespie, Charlie Parker, and vibraphonist Milt Jackson.

LESSON 29
TECHNIQUE/THEORY

Listen to "Stop It" and then play along with the recording. Try to match the vibraphone part. Notice that the comping rhythm changes during the solos. At the head, you will play three comping patterns. For the solo choruses, use the same chords, and follow your ear to match the new rhythm.

First Comping Pattern **Second Comping Pattern** **Third Comping Pattern**

SHARP-NINTH CHORDS (♯9)

The chord in the third comping pattern has a different sound than any chord we have seen so far. It is a variation of an **E7** chord that includes the sharp-ninth scale degree. Its chord symbol is **E7(♯9)**.

To understand how this chord works, start by playing an **E7** chord:

Now, play the notes one by one, and add the ninth. Add each note slowly, holding the pedal down so that you can hear the notes ringing together. Listen for the added richness and color that the ninth adds to the chord sound.

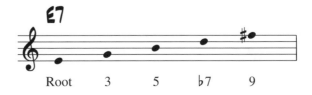

Root   3   5   ♭7   9

Since the chord symbol says (#9), raise that ninth by half a step. The F-sharp becomes F-double-sharp, or G.

Root   3   5   ♭7   #9 or #9

The voicing of this chord used on the recording of "Stop It" omits the fifth. This creates an open, dissonant sound, which is also very common in funk styles.

VOICING PRACTICE

Listen to the sound quality of E7(#9), compared to the other chords in "Stop It."

VOICE LEADING PRACTICE

Practice different voice leading for these chords, beginning on different inversions of A–7. When you play this tune with your own band, you will choose inversions and registers based on which other instruments are present, and what parts they are playing. Practicing a variety of options will help you become more versatile and creative.

PRACTICE TIP

When you are learning new chords and new tunes, practice them "out of time,"
moving from one chord to the next without playing rhythms. This is also a good way
to experiment with different voicings and fingerings.

LESSON 30
LEARNING THE GROOVE

HOOKING UP TO STOP-TIME BLUES

LISTEN **39** PLAY

Listen to "Stop It." This jazz cymbal beat is at the heart of jazz rhythm. The "spang spang a-lang" cymbal beat is unique to jazz, and it has been its primary pattern since the 1940s. Its underlying pulse is the same as the shuffle. This pattern has accompanied Louis Armstrong, Count Basie, Miles Davis, John Coltrane, Duke Ellington, and thousands of other jazz artists.

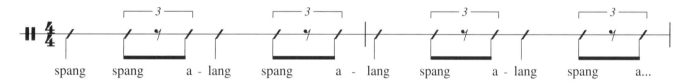

In stop time, the groove is punctuated by *stop-time kicks*. These are rhythmic figures, usually just one or two beats long, that punctuate the melody. That is why it is called "stop time"—the melody "stops" or rests. It is very important that you keep an accurate pulse through these areas where you do not play. Since the accented eighth note is an anticipated third beat, it makes sense to start counting on 4.

LISTEN **40** PLAY

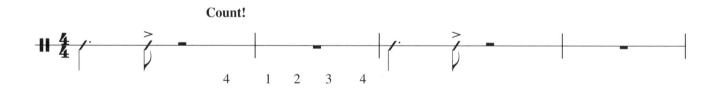

Let's look at the comping rhythm for the stop time melody chorus. Find the pulse and tap quarter notes with your left hand and swing eighth notes with your right hand.

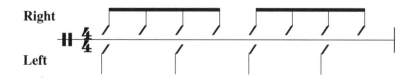

Next, accent the first and fourth eighth notes.

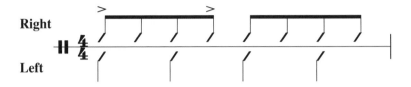

Then tap only the accented notes.

IMPROVISATION CHORUSES

During the solos, the rhythm section *plays time*. The drums play a steady beat and the bass walks. The comping patterns span two measures. Since the vibraphone is soloing here, only the keyboard and guitar play this comping part on the recording.

LISTEN **41** P L A Y

On this exercise, tap quarter notes with your left hand, and the top line with your right hand. Practice until you can "feel" where the comping rhythm's three attacks go.

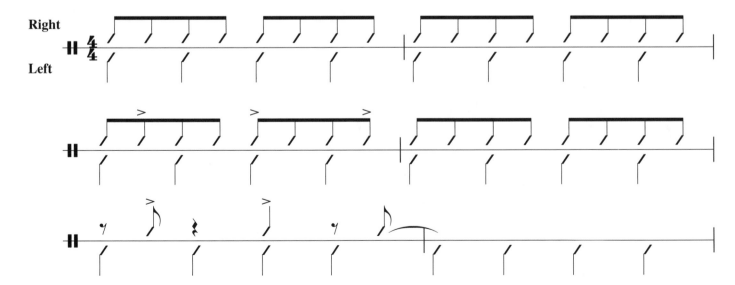

LESSON 31
IMPROVISATION

FORM AND ARRANGEMENT

Listen to "Stop It," and try to figure out the form and arrangement by ear. Check your answer against the summary at the end of this chapter.

LISTEN **39** P L A Y

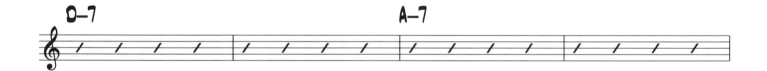

IDEAS FOR IMPROVISING

Scale: A Blues

Use the A blues scale to improvise over this tune.

CALL AND RESPONSE

1. Echo each phrase, exactly as you hear it.
2. Improvise an answer to each phrase. Imitate the sound and rhythmic feel of the phrase you hear, and use the notes from the A blues scale.

LISTEN **42** PLAY

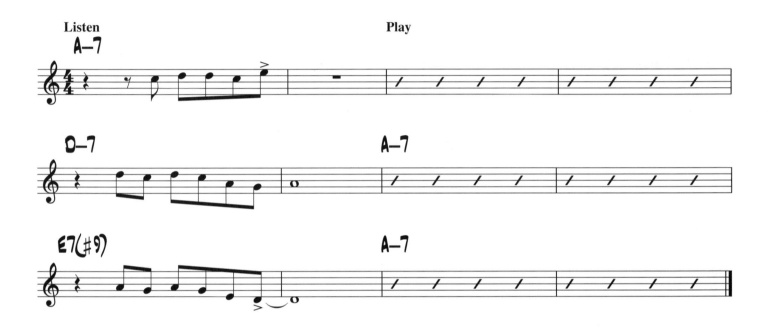

LISTEN **43** PLAY

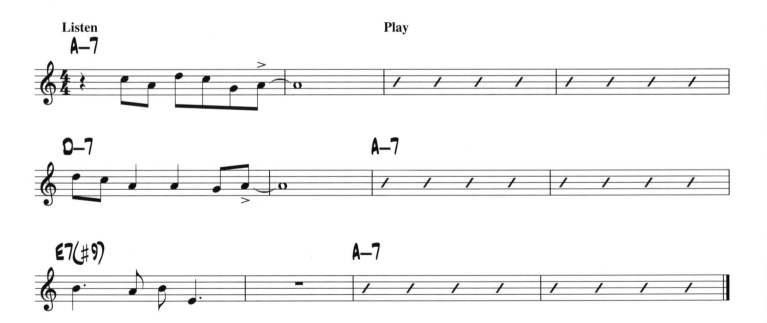

Write out a few of your own ideas. Use the A blues scale.

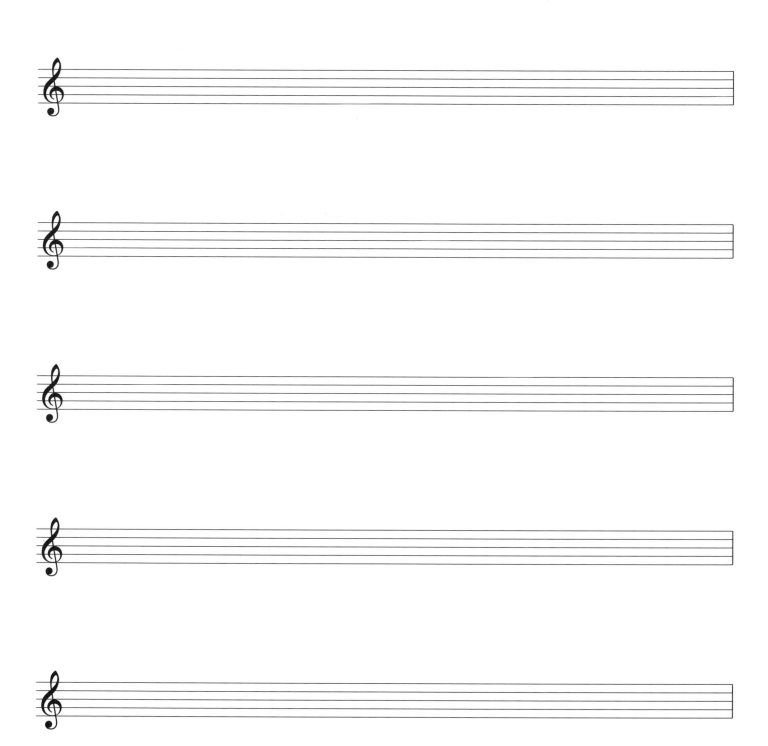

LISTEN **44** PLAY

Create a one-chorus solo using any techniques you have learned. Memorize your solo, and practice it along with the recording.

LESSON 32
READING

VIBRAPHONE PART

D.C. AL ⊕ From the beginning, and take the coda. Jump to the very first measure of the tune, and play from there. When you reach the first coda symbol, skip ahead to the next coda symbol (at the end). This is similar to the "**D.S. AL CODA**," but instead of going to a sign, go to the first measure of the tune.

Play "Stop It" along with the recording, and read from the written vibraphone part.

LISTEN **44** PLAY

STOP IT
VIBRAPHONE PART

BY MATT MARVUGLIO

LEAD SHEET

Play "Stop It" from the lead sheet. Use your own comping part.

STOP IT

By Matt Marvuglio

CHAPTER VIII
DAILY PRACTICE ROUTINE

TECHNIQUE/THEORY

Inversion Practice

Play this inversion exercise along with the recording.

LISTEN **44** PLAY

Pentatonic Practice 1

Even though pentatonic scales have five notes, they are often used in groups of four, as this grouping will fit better into $\frac{4}{4}$ time—groupings of fours, eights, etc.

Practice these 4-note groupings slowly until the shapes become comfortable. Notice that the suggested fingering treats each group as a separate phrase and makes no attempt to connect one group to another. Try a variety of stickings.

Pentatonic Practice 2

As these groups become more comfortable, try to increase the speed. When you are ready, play them as eighth notes with the recording.

Pentatonic Practice 3

Below is a 4-measure melody that uses only notes from the A minor pentatonic scale. If this phrase is stated three times, it will follow the blues form of twelve measures divided into three 4-measure phrases. Practicing this will help you develop a sense of the form and phrasing of the blues.

Create your own 4-measure phrase that repeats over the blues form. Use the A blues scale.

IMPROVISATION

Solo Rhythms

Use the following rhythms and the A blues scale to create solo licks. Practice them along with the recording. Use the same rhythm to create several different licks.

Improvisation Licks

These licks are typical of what you might create for a stop-time solo. Notice the use of triplets and syncopations. Practice each one until you can play it easily. Try a variety of stickings until you find one that is comfortable for you.

Improvisation Practice

Improvise on "Stop It." Play several choruses using the blues scale, chord tones, licks from the melody, and any other techniques you have learned. Develop your solo, and then practice it along with the recording.

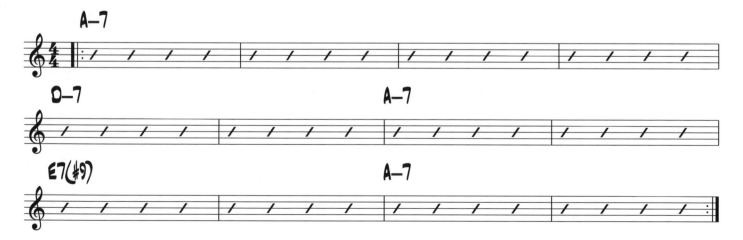

SOLO PRACTICE

Practice this solo to "Stop It" along with the recording.

MEMORIZE

Create your own comping part and improvised solo to "Stop It." Practice it along with the recording, and memorize it.

SUMMARY

PLAY "STOP IT" WITH YOUR OWN BAND!

FINAL REMARKS

Congratulations on completing the *Berklee Practice Method.* You now have a good idea of the role of the vibraphonist in the band, and have command of the eight grooves and time feels of these tunes. The chords, voicings, and harmonic progressions that you have learned are important and useful parts of your musical vocabulary. In addition, you have tools and ideas for creating your own comping patterns and solos. This is a great start!

What to do next? Play along with your favorite recordings. Find records that you hear other musicians talking about. Learn these tunes, grooves, and comping patterns. There is a good reason that musicians talk about certain bands, albums, or vibists. Continue your theory, reading, and technique work. Investigate chord scales and modes. Learn all your key signatures (major and minor), scales, and arpeggios.

Develop your concept of what it means to play vibraphone. Realize how important you are as a vibraphonist in a band. You have a big responsibility, taking care of both the groove and the harmony. It is a powerful position.

Play your vibraphone every day, by yourself and with others, and get the sound in your body.

Playing music requires a lot of practice, discipline, and constant study. Remember, though, that we play music because we enjoy it. It should be fun, and you should be sure that you don't take it so seriously that you lose sight of the fun.

Keep the beat!

—Ed

Get Your Band Together with the
BERKLEE PRACTICE METHOD
from Berklee Press

Make your band better, or prepare yourself to join one! This sensational series lets you improve your intuitive sense of timing and improvisation, develop your technique and reading ability, and master your role in the groove. Play along with a Berklee faculty band on the accompanying CD, then play with your own band!

Alto Sax by Jim Odgren, Bill Pierce, and the Berklee Faculty
ISBN 0-634-00795-5 • HL50449437 Book/CD $14.95

Bass by Rich Appleman, John Repucci, and the Berklee Faculty
ISBN 0-634-00650-9 • HL50449427 Book/CD $14.95

Drum Set by Ron Savage, Casey Scheuerell, and the Berklee Faculty
ISBN 0-634-00652-5 • HL50449429 Book/CD $14.95

Guitar by Larry Baione and the Berklee Faculty
ISBN 0-634-00649-5 • HL50449426 Book/CD $14.95

Keyboard by Paul Schmeling, Russell Hoffmann, and the Berklee Faculty
ISBN 0-634-00651-7 • HL50449428 Book/CD $14.95

Tenor Sax by Jim Odgren, Bill Pierce, and the Berklee Faculty
ISBN 0-634-00789-0 • HL50449431 Book/CD $14.95

Trombone by Jeff Galindo and the Berklee Faculty
ISBN 0-634-00791-2 • HL50449433 Book/CD $14.95

Trumpet by Tiger Okoshi, Charles Lewis, and the Berklee Faculty
ISBN 0-634-00790-4 • HL50449432 Book/CD $14.95

Vibraphone by Ed Saindon and the Berklee Faculty
ISBN 0-634-00794-7 • HL50449436 Book/CD $14.95

Violin by Matt Glaser, Mimi Rabson, and the Berklee Faculty
ISBN 0-634-00792-0 • HL50449434 Book/CD $14.95

 **berklee press**

For more information about Berklee Press or Berklee College of Music, contact us:
1140 Boylston Street
Boston, MA 02215-3693
www.berkleepress.com

Visit your local music dealer or bookstore, or go to www.berkleepress.com

Prices and availability subject to change without notice.

 **berklee press**

Berklee Press books and DVDs are available wherever music books are sold. Go to www.berkleepress.com or call 866-BERKLEE for a complete catalog of Berklee Press products.

DISTRIBUTED BY

HAL•LEONARD®
CORPORATION
7777 W. BLUEMOUND RD. P.O. BOX 13819
MILWAUKEE, WISCONSIN 53213

THE BEST OF BERKLEE PRESS

GUITAR

Guitar Books by William Leavitt
Berklee Basic Guitar - Phase 1
0-634-01333-5 Book $7.95

Berklee Basic Guitar - Phase 2
0-7935-5526-4 Book $7.95

Classical Studies for Pick-Style Guitar
0-634-01339-4 Book $9.95

A Modern Method for Guitar
Volume 1: Beginner
0-87639-013-0 Book/CD $22.95

0-87639-014-9 Book $14.95

Volume 2: Intermediate
0-87639-016-5 Book/CD $22.95

0-87639-015-7 Book $14.95

Volume 3: Advanced
0-87639-017-3 Book $14.95

1-2-3 Complete
0-87639-011-4 Book $29.95

Melodic Rhythms for Guitar
0-634-01332-7 Book $14.95

Reading Studies for Guitar
0-634-01335-1 Book $14.95

Advanced Reading Studies for Guitar
0-634-01337-8 Book $14.95

Jim Kelly Guitar Workshop Series
Jim Kelly's Guitar Workshop
0-7935-8572-4 Book/CD $14.95

0-634-00865-X DVD $29.95
More Guitar Workshop
0-7935-9454-4 Book/CD $14.95
0-634-00648-7 VHS $19.95

BASS

The Bass Player's Handbook
by Greg Mooter
0-634-02300-4 Book $24.95

Chord Studies for Electric Bass
by Rich Appleman
0-634-01646-6 Book $14.95

Reading Contemporary Electric Bass
by Rich Appleman
0-634-01338-6 Book $14.95

Rock Bass Lines
by Joe Santerre
0-634-01432-3 Book/CD $19.95

Slap Bass Lines
by Joe Santerre
0-634-02144-3 Book/CD $19.95

KEYBOARD

Solo Jazz Piano
by Neil Olmstead
0-634-00761-0 Book/CD $39.95

Hammond Organ Complete
by Dave Limina
0-634-01433-1 Book/CD $24.95

A Modern Method for Keyboard
by James Progris
0-634-01329-7 Vol. 1: Beginner
0-634-01330-0 Vol. 2: Intermediate
0-634-01830-2 Vol. 3: Advanced
Book $14.95 (each)

DRUMS AND PERCUSSION

Beyond the Backbeat
by Larry Finn
0-634-00701-7 Book/CD $19.95

Brazilian Rhythms for Drum Set and Percussion
By Alberto Netto
0-634-02143-5 Book/CD $29.95

Drum Set Warm-Ups
by Rod Morgenstein
0-634-00965-6 Book $12.95

Mastering the Art of Brushes
by Jon Hazilla
0-634-00962-1 Book/CD $19.95

The Reading Drummer
by Dave Vose
0-634-00961-3 Book $9.95

Rudiment Grooves for Drum Set
By Rick Considine
0-87639-009-2 Book/CD $19.95

SAXOPHONE

Books by Joseph Viola

Creative Reading Studies for Saxophone
0-634-01334-3 Book $14.95

Technique of the Saxophone
0-7935-5409-8 Volume 1: Scale Studies
0-7935-5412-8 Volume 2: Chord Studies
0-7935-5428-4 Volume 3: Rhythm Studies
Book $14.95 (each)

TOOLS FOR DJs

Turntable Technique: The Art of the DJ
by Stephen Webber
0-87639-010-6 Book/2-Record Set$34.95
0-87639-038-6 DVD $24.95
0-87639-039-4 VHS $24.95

Turntable Basics
by Stephen Webber
0-634-02612-7 Book $9.95

MUSIC BUSINESS

How to Get a Job in the Music & Recording Industry
by Keith Hatschek
0-634-01868-X Book $24.95

**Mix Masters: Platinum Engineers Reveal
Their Secrets for Success**
by Maureen Droney
0-87639-019-X Book $24.95

The Musician's Internet
by Peter Spellman
0-634-03586-X Book $24.95

The New Music Therapist's Handbook, Second Edition
by Suzanne B. Hanser
0-634-00645-2 Book $29.95

The Self-Promoting Musician
by Peter Spellman
0-634-00644-4 Book $24.95

SONGWRITING / ARRANGING / VOICE

Arranging for Large Jazz Ensemble
by Ken Pullig
0-634-03656-4 Book/CD $39.95

Complete Guide to Film Scoring
by Richard Davis
0-634-00636-3 Book $24.95

The Contemporary Singer
By Anne Peckham
0-634-00797-1 Book/CD $24.95

Essential Ear Training
by Steve Prosser
0-634-00640-1 Book $14.95

Jazz Composition: Theory and Practice
By Ted Pease
0-87639-001-7 Book/CD $39.95

Melody in Songwriting
by Jack Perricone
0-634-00638-X Book $19.95

Modern Jazz Voicings
by Ted Pease and Ken Pullig
0-634-01443-9 Book/CD $24.95

Music Notation
by Mark McGrain
0-7935-0847-9 Book $19.95

Reharmonization Techniques
by Randy Felts
0-634-01585-0 Book $29.95

The Songs of John Lennon
by John Stevens
0-634-01795-0 Book $24.95

The Songwriter's Workshop: Melody
by Jimmy Kachulis
0-634-02659-3 Book $24.95

Songwriting: Essential Guide to Lyric Form & Structure
by Pat Pattison
0-7935-1180-1 Book $14.95

Songwriting: Essential Guide to Rhyming
by Pat Pattison
0-7935-1181-X Book $14.95

BERKLEE PRACTICE METHOD

0-634-00650-9 **Bass** by Rich Appleman and John Repucci
0-634-00652-5 **Drum Set** by Ron Savage and Casey Scheuerell
0-634-00649-5 **Guitar** by Larry Baione
0-634-00651-7 **Keyboard** by Russell Hoffmann and Paul Schmeling
0-634-00795-5 **Alto Sax** by Jim Odgren and Bill Pierce
0-634-00798-0 **Tenor Sax** by Jim Odgren and Bill Pierce
0-634-00791-2 **Trombone** by Jeff Galindo
0-634-00790-4 **Trumpet** by Tiger Okoshi and Charles Lewis
0-634-00794-7 **Vibraphone** by Ed Saindon
0-634-00792-0 **Violin** by Matt Glaser and Mimi Rabson
Book/CD $14.95 (each)

BERKLEE INSTANT SERIES

0-634-01667-9 **Bass** by Danny Morris
0-634-02602-X **Drum Set** by Ron Savage
0-634-02951-7 **Guitar** by Tomo Fujita
0-634-03141-4 **Keyboard** by Paul Schmeling and Dave Limina
Book/CD $14.95 (each)

IMPROVISATION

Blues Improvisation Complete Series
by Jeff Harrington
0-634-01530-3 Bb Instruments
0-634-01532-X C Bass Instruments
0-634-00647-9 C Treble Instruments
0-634-01531-7 Eb Instruments
Book/CD $19.95 (each)

A Guide to Jazz Improvisation Series
by John LaPorta
0-634-00700-9 C Instruments
0-634-00762-9 Bb Instruments
0-634-00763-7 Eb Instruments
0-634-00764-5 Bass Clef
Book $16.95 (each)

MUSIC TECHNOLOGY

Arranging in the Digital World
by Corey Allen
0-634-00634-7 Book/MIDI Disk $19.95

Finale: An Easy Guide to Music Notation
by Tom Rudolph and Vince Leonard
0-634-01666-0 Book/CD-ROM $59.95

**Producing in the Home Studio with
Pro Tools Second Edition**
by David Franz
0-87639-008-4 Book/CD-ROM $34.95

Recording in the Digital World
by Tom Rudolph and Vince Leonard
0-634-01324-6 Book $29.95

POP CULTURE

Inside the Hits
by Wayne Wadhams
0-634-01430-7 Book $29.95

Masters of Music: Conversations with Berklee Greats
by Mark Small and Andrew Taylor
0-634-00642-8 Book $24.95

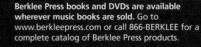

Study Online

with
Berklee
college *of*
music

Now that you've read the book, here's a great opportunity to get some hands-on instruction with renowned Berklee College of Music professors. Our instructor-led online courses are the perfect next step in continuing your musical education. Current course offerings focus on areas including:

- **Production**
- **Writing**
- **Performance**
- **Education**
- **Music Business**

Here's what our online students have said about Berkleemusic's courses:

"The convenience of working at home is so great! Being able to take a course like this from an expert is a tremendous bonus for those who don't live in a city accessible to physical classes."

— D. Boughton

"I feel that my questions were not only answered but new ones were raised and those in turn were answered. It was really remarkable."

— D. Sprunger

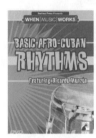

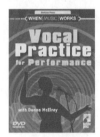